QUILTING, PATCHWORK & APPLIQUÉ

CAROLINE CRABTREE
CHRISTINE SHAW

QUILTING, PATCHWORK & APPLIQUÉ

A WORLD GUIDE

with 520 illustrations,
504 in color

Thames & Hudson

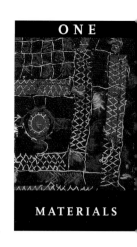

ONE

MATERIALS

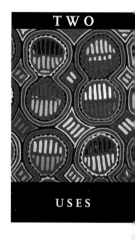

TWO

USES

THREE

CONSTRUCTION

FOR PHILIP, ALICE AND EMMA; AND FOR GEORGIA

PAGE 1: *Child's tunic, Turkestan, pieced from cotton and ikat silk.*

PAGE 2: *Worn batik fabrics, from Indonesia, made into a quilt using very simple block piecing; such items are sold to tourists.*

PAGE 3: *Early 20th-century English quilt. The design of an eight-point Star within a Star quilt is attributed to Elizabeth Sanderson.*

PAGE 5: *North American hand-appliqué block design known as the Rose of Sharon.*

PAGE 6, ABOVE, RIGHT: *Wool jacket, appliquéd with dancing figures, from Mexico; almost certainly made in the 1950s for the tourist market.*

LEFT: *Cotton Log Cabin quilt, early 20th century, with Turkey Red printed cotton border.*

BOTTOM RIGHT: *Asafo military company flag, with pieced Union flag and appliquéd dragon, Ghana.*

P. 7, ABOVE, LEFT: *Frame quilt with a central panel worked in nine patchwork blocks, which together show an eight-point Star within a Star, early 20th century.*

BELOW, LEFT: *Cradle cloth, made by the Banjara of central and southern India, with appliqué and reverse appliqué.*

RIGHT: *Camel trapping, from Central Asia, decorated with pieced squares of cotton and silk ikat fabrics.*

ACKNOWLEDGEMENTS

The American Museum in Britain, Meg Andrews (www.meg-andrews.com), Sue Aspinall, Caroline Bevan, Gene Bowen, The British Museum, London, Melanie Brown and the staff of Afghan Aid (www.afghanaid.org.uk), Tessa Bunney, Mary Cooper, Jean Douglas, Esther Fitzgerald (www.estherfitzgerald.com), Jim and Dianne Gaffney of Textile Traders (www.textiletechniques.co.uk), John Gillow, Joss Graham and all the staff of the Joss Graham Gallery, Denise Holtby, Jennifer Hughes, Department of South-East Asian Studies, Hull University, Jan Jefferson of JJN Amish Quilts, Glenn Jowitt, Antonia Lovelace of Leeds City Museum, Polly Medley, Anna Miskin of Tana Mana, Brigid Ockleton, Margaret Pettit, Quilters Guild of Great Britain, Ron Simpson, Kate Smith, Sheila Smith, Sally Stone, The Victoria and Albert Museum, London, York Castle Museum, Whitby Museum.

Design by David Fordham

© 2007 Thames & Hudson Ltd, London

First published in hardcover in 2007 in the United States of America by Thames & Hudson Inc., 500 Fifth Avenue, New York, New York 10110

thamesandhudsonusa.com

Library of Congress Catalog Card Number 2007921452

ISBN 978-0-500-51373-6

Printed and bound in Singapore by CS Graphics

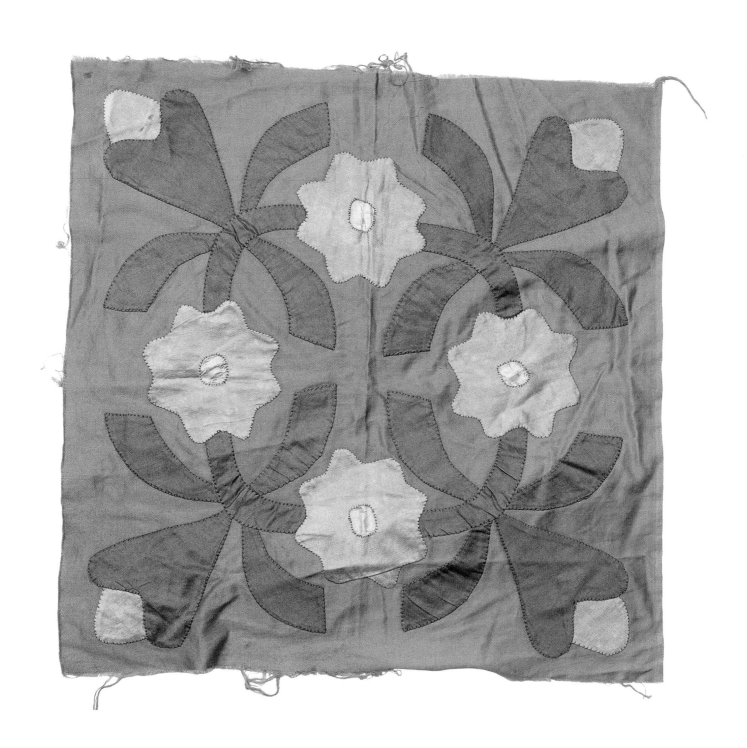

CONTENTS

INTRODUCTION

ATCHWORK IS created when new fabric is cut and re-shaped into multi-coloured, multi-patterned cloth, or old fabric pieces are cut and re-stitched to produce a new textile. Quilting uses stitching to hold layers of fabric together and is sometimes utilitarian, but also often very decorative. Appliqué is the cutting and placing of old and new fabric to adorn and decorate. Two or more of the techniques may be combined, for instance, when cloth that is pieced is then quilted, or a pieced or quilted base is further embellished with appliqué.

ABOVE, RIGHT; AND LEFT: Multi-coloured pieced silk chevrons of plain and gauze weave, part of an altar valance found in the Caves of the Thousand Buddhas near Dunhuang in China. It dates from 700–900; Indian canopy constructed from cotton handkerchiefs, produced in Manchester, England, in the 19th century.

BELOW, LEFT: Reverse side of an English Grandmother's Flower Garden quilt top showing the papers used in the construction. The material is tacked over the paper to create the hexagon shape and is joined to another hexagon by overstitching.

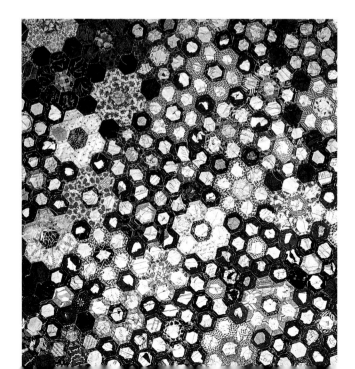

THE PURPOSE OF THIS BOOK

HERE ARE many books that concentrate on a specific patchwork, quilting or appliqué technique, or look at quilts, usually European or North American bed quilts, from a historical viewpoint, but none, to our knowledge, deals with the subject from a worldwide perspective, or shows the diversity of materials used, or the range of objects produced. Not just cloth of wool, linen, cotton or silk, but felt, leather, fish skin and plant fibres have been and are still used. While today the techniques of patchwork and quilting are usually thought of only in terms of bedding, the range of objects made using patchwork, quilting and appliqué includes items for household use, clothing, political protest panels, animal trappings and military, religious and ritual objects. In all parts of the world textiles have played a significant role through rites of passage. Quilting, patchwork and appliquéd objects have been made for births, christenings, circumcisions, weddings and funerals.

By showing items from many places side by side we invite comparison and an awareness of the diversity of objects being made and the range of techniques involved. With the illustrations we aim to show the development of regional styles and their place in cultural identity. The techniques in patchwork, quilting and appliqué are many and varied and your journey through this book will provide you with information to aid identification.

LEFT: *Detail of folded patchwork on a Lahu woman's coat, Thailand.*

RIGHT; AND BELOW, RIGHT: *Intricate silk hexagon quilt design, from England, made over papers using dress silks and silk ribbons, 19th century; detail of an English 20th-century scrap quilt of printed cotton with a random design.*

THE HISTORY OF PATCHWORK

BEFORE THE mass production of textiles during the Industrial Revolution in Europe in the 19th century, cloth was a precious commodity, to be used sparingly. Small left-over pieces of precious silk or velvet or other costly cloth, or skin, would be remade into a larger whole, or the useable parts of worn clothing would be cut up and reused to make new clothing or household objects. The reusing of worn garments is by nature a craft of necessity and poverty, so the objects made tended to be used until they disintegrated through wear. The *boro* – which translates as rags – textiles of Japan are perhaps the best example of this utility and necessity, though the once humble cloths and garments are now regarded as collectable art objects.

The perishable nature of the materials, especially when the fabric was already weakened with use, means very little patchwork has survived; perhaps one of the oldest pieces of patchwork and appliqué, dating from the 11 century BC, is the funeral tent of the Egyptian Queen, Istemkeb, currently in the Egyptian Museum in Cairo. This has dyed patchwork squares and decorative applied borders made from gazelle hide. During the 1920s a large collection of ancient textiles was discovered in the Caves of the Thousand Buddhas, situated in China, on the Silk Route. Among the finds were several pieces of mosaic patchwork, a large votive hanging made from many coloured rectangles of silk and damask, patchwork tops for banners and a small silk purse in squares and rectangles, all believed to be around 1,200 years old. Some of these objects show an unusual method of construction; they are oversewn on the wrong side in a manner similar to a technique known today as English piecing. In Europe, two early fragments of Anglo-Saxon work, dating from the 8th to early 9th centuries, are to be found at Maaseik, Limburg in Belgium. They were made in the south of England and one of them, a religious vestment, is constructed from many fragments of silk textiles.

The first and only reference to an early patchwork bed cover – the use of patchwork that springs most readily to mind today – is in a book of French poems dating from the 12th or 13th centuries, where it is described as a cover of checkerboard design with two sorts of silk cloth.

In Sweden bed quilts dating back to the 15th century have survived, as well as a few examples from the 17th century, although it was not until the British East India Trading Company, founded in 1601, followed by other similar trading companies in France, Portugal and the Netherlands, began to import large quantities of fine printed cottons from India to Europe that pieced work, using new as well as worn cloth, became more commonplace. In the English novel *Gulliver's Travels*, published in 1726, there is a remark that Gulliver's clothes 'looked like the patchwork made by the ladies in England'.

By the 19th century patchwork as a domestic craft was widespread throughout Europe and North America; there is evidence of patchwork being made in Australia, Africa and India, though it is thought that this was mostly due to the influence of European settlers. In the Far East, Korea, in particular, has its own indigenous style of patchwork; *pojagi* was once the economical use of left-over pieces of costly sheer gauze, but has now become an art form, copied and used by international couturiers.

A HISTORY OF QUILTING

THERE IS no doubt that quilting is ancient in origin. It is thought to have its origins in Asia and to have travelled by the Oriental trade routes to other parts of Asia and Europe. Whether the art began in India, Persia or Egypt, quilting as protection for animals and worn beneath armour was known in Japan, India and Africa. It is considered to have been brought into Europe in the 11th to the 13th centuries during the Crusades by the soldiers returning from North Africa and the Middle East. Many of the knights returning home wore quilted garments beneath their armour and quilted linen caps under heavy metal helmets. The importance of this use of quilting is demonstrated by the setting up, in 1272, of the Guild of Linen Armourers in England. It existed until the 15th century when

TOP LEFT: *Applied strips decorate the skirt of this woman from Kutch, Gujarat, north-west India.*

CENTRE: *Two Lisu tunics, from Asia, with machine-stitched, folded strip patchwork around the neck and shoulders. The body of the female tunic is usually blue or green and the sleeves are red.*

OPPOSITE, FAR RIGHT: *Young boy from Afghanistan wearing a* chapan *of quilted cotton; the* chapan *is the ubiquitous garment of Central Asia, worn by young and old, rich and poor.*

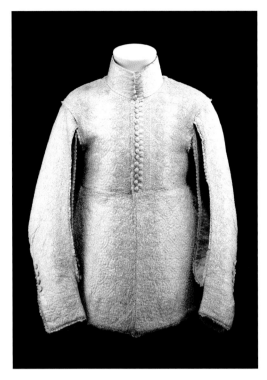

the guild became the Merchant Taylors' Company. Domestic quilting in Europe of the 11th, 12th and 13th centuries does not seem to have had the same importance as quilted armour of the period.

By the end of the 14th century examples of domestic quilting are more in evidence. Three known examples of bed quilts, thought to be Sicilian in origin, have survived; one of these is in the collection of the Victoria and Albert Museum in London and is known as the Tristram bed cover. It is a Narrative quilt, telling the story of Tristram and Isolde and is made of linen with stuffed and corded figures outlined in back stitch as well as background quilting. Corded quilting is a labour-intensive decorative technique intended for wealthy people and was well known in Italy, which had strong trading links with the Middle East. It is possible that the technique began in the Middle East, since it gives texture and body to the item without creating the thick warm layer typical of wadded quilting.

Other examples of Narrative quilts are the *kanthas* of West Bengal and Bangladesh. The *kantha*, literally 'patched cloth', combines quilting and embroidery and was originally made of layers of old sari fabric. The Portuguese, who settled in Bengal after Vasco da Gama chartered a sea route to India in 1498, planned to send Indian needleworkers to Lisbon in 1511, but the ship sank off Sumatra, though it is likely that other needleworkers travelled to Lisbon to create quilts in the *kantha* style. This style of embroidery and quilting became known as *colcha* and was in turn exported to South America. Alongside the *kanthas*, quilted pictorial bed covers worked in silk, often incorporating hunting scenes of figures in European dress, were made in Bengal for the European market. These 'Bengalla' quilts were known in Europe prior to the start of English trade in India. The earliest known reference to their sale is a report of an auction in London in 1618.

Top left: *Quilted doublet made in the 17th century from glazed linen. Initially these were armorial garments, but later became everyday wear, England.*

Left: *Appliquéd and quilted daffodil quilt made in North America and sent to northern England as a wedding gift in the 1920s.*

Simultaneously, the craft was popular in most European countries, in the Orient, in Persia and in North, East and West Africa. From the 16th century onwards there is a wealth of evidence of quilted clothing, some from surviving garments and some from paintings. Protective animal trappings and body armour of quilted cotton were made in Sudan during the 19th century and is still made and worn, though today solely for ceremonial use. The quilted petticoat was still being worn, in some places, up to the beginning of the 20th century, as a working garment.

A HISTORY OF APPLIQUÉ

SOME OF the earliest appliqués have been found in the Middle East, Turkey, Egypt and southern Siberia. Wall hangings and saddle trappings with appliquéd decoration have been discovered during excavations of burial sites dating from the 5th century BC. Felt appliqué was produced by the nomadic tribes of Central Asia and Siberia, while in Siberia and Northern America fish, particularly salmon, skin was used for the appliquéd decoration of bags and clothing. Beautiful appliquéd hangings decorated with plants, animal, birds and dancing figures have been found in Egyptian burial sites, dating from AD 300 to 1000. During the Middle Ages, throughout Europe, appliqué was used on household furnishings; it was a cheap – because it was quick to produce – substitute for embroidery and tapestry. It was also used for banners and was adopted by knights on their surcoats to provide some means of distinguishing between friend and foe. Since textiles were scarce, appliqué became, like patchwork, a means of utilizing small pieces of precious fabrics or reusing the good parts of worn cloth.

ABOVE, LEFT; AND ABOVE, RIGHT: *Detail showing intricate inlaid appliqué patterns made by using the woollen material from soldiers' and sailors' uniforms, England; Mongolian family group: their traditional dress is decorated with applied strips that emphasize the shaping of the garment.*

BELOW; AND BOTTOM: *German 14th-century appliquéd hanging telling the tale of Tristan and Isolde; Chinese boy's shoes, with an applied fish motif symbolizing plenty.*

In Europe, by the 13th and 14th centuries applied work was mainly used on ecclesiastical vestments and altar frontals, but by the 16th century was just as frequently used for secular hangings, canopies, bed curtains, valances and coverlets. In France and Italy leather or stiffened fabrics such as velvet or heavy brocade were used for the appliqué on furnishings and saddle trappings; fabrics were stiffened with glue and paper and sewn onto the background with a cord couched around the edge. This method was also used to sew on

leather shapes. Following the discovery of the sea route to India and the greatly increased trade with India, printed and painted chintzes began to arrive in Europe in around 1606. This new imported fabric was cut up and the individual floral motifs stitched to fabric. The technique was known as Broderie Perse, named after the Persian embroidery brought to Europe in the 12th and 13th centuries.

Felt has been used in appliqué for many centuries, its unique non-fraying properties making it ideal for cutting intricate patterns. It continues to be used by nomadic tribesmen in Central Asia for floor coverings, bags and camel trappings and is also used in Hungary and Poland for intricately cut and applied decoration. The Resht region of Iran is famous for a particular style of inlaid appliqué made from felt, cotton or wool. Leather and skin has similar properties to felt and was used for appliquéd decoration in Eastern Europe, Siberia and Northern America.

ABOVE, RIGHT: *Indian wall hanging made by the Rabari of Kutch. The very typical design is, most unusually, made with minute pieces of applied fabric rather than embroidery.*

LEFT: *Palm leaf and cane hat decorated with cloth appliqué and beads; made for tourists at the Sarawak handicraft centre in Malaysia.*

RIGHT: *Cloth printed with a design typical of the finely worked appliqué of the Hmong tribe of Thailand.*

BELOW, LEFT: *Hmong children from Thailand wearing traditional festival clothing made using intricate appliqué techniques.*

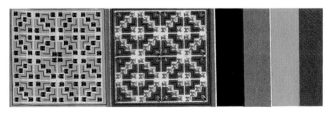

Appliqué has not always been for the purpose of adornment – in its earliest form it was surely functional, the strengthening of a worn place with another piece of cloth. An example is the garments of the Sudanese army of the Mahdi who in the late 19th century covered their uniforms in applied pieces of rough cloth, to symbolize the poverty and humility of the followers of this religious leader following the tradition of the Sufi religious orders. Later, as the army increased in number and became formalized, the garments also became more of a formal uniform, of new cloth decorated with symbolic applied patches.

CONCLUSION

WHILE PATCHWORK, quilting and appliqué all began as a functional solution to the need to conserve or reuse fabric, to strengthen worn places or add extra substance and warmth, these stitched techniques are now used to decorate, adorn and embellish, and their functional purpose has mostly become of secondary importance.

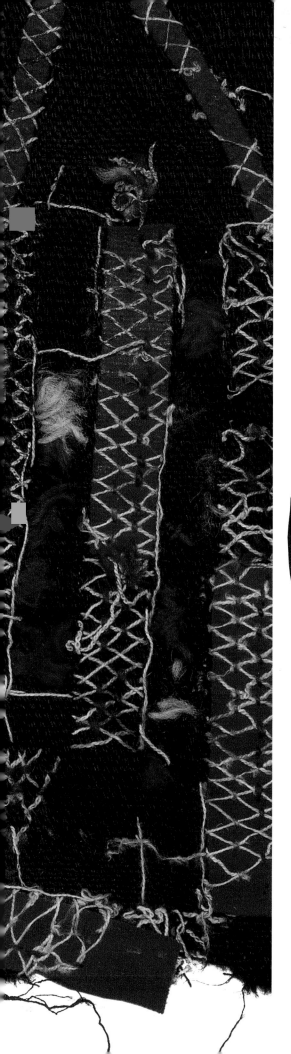

MATERIALS

LEFT; AND RIGHT: *Detail of a Bedawi woman's head cloth of appliquéd wool and embroidery, Tunisia; fragment of the border of a gold-covered goatskin applied to cotton, from Indonesia.*

CENTRE: *European sleeve band of silk with painted appliquéd motifs, late 19th century.*

BELOW, LEFT; AND BELOW, RIGHT: *Chinese woman's collar to be applied to a dress; West African ceremonial dance skirt of patch-work with raffia cloth squares.*

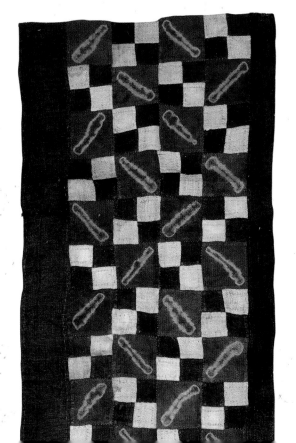

INTRODUCTION

BEFORE THE development of spinning and weaving, man discovered how to use animal hides and skins, to interlace vegetable fibres and to pulp bark in water to form a textile. Early peoples developed four main fibres: wool, flax and linen, cotton and silk.

WOOL

ABOVE: HOUSEHOLD ITEMS DECORATED WITH APPLIQUÉ, GUJARAT, NORTH-WESTERN INDIA.

IT IS thought that sheep were domesticated in Afghanistan and Mesopotamia three thousand years ago. Various species developed, differences in climate and available pasture combining to produce the widely differing varieties, although systematic breeding to make finer qualities of wool is not recorded until early Roman times. Plucking was the typical Bronze Age method of collecting the fibre; the change from plucking to shearing provided a fleece in one piece instead of tufts. After shearing, wool was cleaned and combed or carded and often dyed before being spun. Anthropologists differ in their views of whether weaving originated in China, India, Mesopotamia or Egypt, but it is thought to have begun before 5000 BC and then spread through Europe and Asia.

ABOVE: *Rolling felt at a roadside stall, Turkey.*

BELOW, FAR LEFT: *Detail of inlay appliqué in fine wool cloth from Resht, Iran. Resht is a centre of professional inlay workers.*

BELOW, CENTRE: Chakla, *from Rajasthan in north-western India, with pieced borders and a printed cotton centre.*

BELOW, RIGHT: *Flowers and saw-toothed appliqué decorate a wall hanging from Rajasthan, north-western India.*

FLAX AND LINEN

FLAX IS said to be one of the first fibres of plant origin to have been used by man. It was cultivated , spun and woven well before 2500 BC in both Europe and Ancient Egypt. The annual variety of flax (*Linum usitatissimum*) was first found in the Orient, but the perennial form of flax (*Linium austriacum* or *augustifolium*) was used by early man and was probably superseded by the annual variety at least four thousand years before Christ. Most of the flax products in the ancient world came from Egypt.

COTTON

I N THE ancient world the cotton plant was first cultivated in India, Ethiopia, the Sudan and Senegal, where it was called *carbasus*: the Arabic word cotton is relatively modern. Cotton fabric and threads, some dyed purple, were found before 1500 BC in the Indus Valley around Mohenjo-Daro. The Egyptians liked the appearance of cotton and it was often used with silk or linen threads to produce a mixed textile. Cotton is the most widely used and versatile of textile fibres.

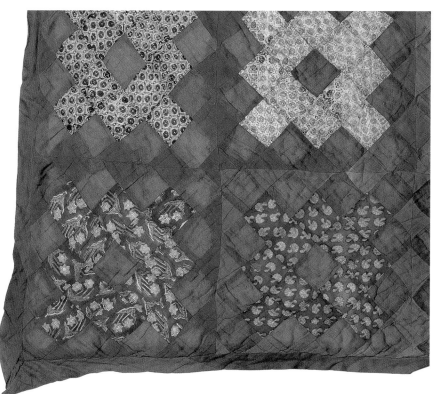

ABOVE, LEFT: *Ainu couple, from Hokkaido in Japan, wearing clothing decorated in the appliquéd pattern typically made by this people.*

LEFT: *Detail of a quilt made in north India in the early 20th century for the European market; it is lightweight cotton gauze filled with cotton fibres.*

BELOW, RIGHT: *Hand-block printed cotton fabrics from Gujarat, north-western India.*

SILK

T HE CULTIVATION of silk in China can be traced back many thousands of years. In the 1st century AD silk was one of the treasures of the East; the manufacture of silk fabric was a jealously guarded secret until the 6th century AD, when it was brought to Asia Minor and Byzantium. In Egypt a piece of coloured wild silk was found dating from the 4th century AD, but silk was rare enough for Coptic weavers to make woollen imitations of the silks as late as the 7th century. Silk is still a luxury fabric.

The textiles made by these early civilizations all show a high degree of expertise and sophistication.

COTTON AND LINEN

Worldwide, cotton is the most important fibre known to man. It is a member of the mallow family, a dark green-leaved bush with deep red-purple blossoms, producing bolls of silky cotton. It is widely grown in sub-tropical regions throughout the world: in the south of North America, the north of South America, North Africa, India, China and

TOP; AND FAR LEFT: *North Country strippy quilt, unusually made from linen rather than cotton sateen, 19th century, England. Traditional quilting patterns follow the design of strips; simple quilt of printed linen furnishing fabric samples, English, early 20th century.*

ABOVE: *Rumal – a ceremonial cloth for covering gifts – made by the Banjara people of India. The embroidered centre is surrounded by pieced sections.*

LEFT: *Small Egyptian linen hanging with applied Pharaonic motifs, early 20th century.*

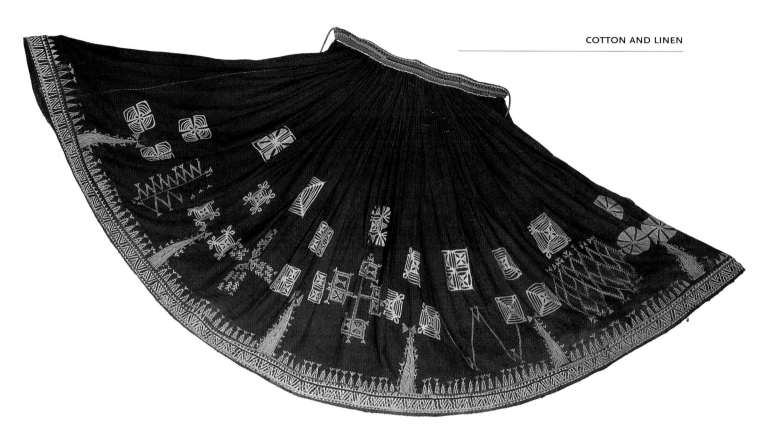

south Russia. The Arabic word cotton is relatively modern, in ancient times it was called carbasus.

Archaeological studies have suggested that cotton was grown in Egypt in around 12000 BC, but the evidence from actual finds shows that fine cotton was being woven in both India and Egypt from 3000 BC and in Peru from around 2300 BC. Fragments of cotton have been found in Native American burial sites in Utah, Texas and Arizona, showing that it was grown there as early as 500 BC.

Trade

COTTON growing and manufacture spread from the ancient sites to the Mediterranean and cotton was carried on the ancient trade routes. By the 10th century fine cottons were being produced in Spain and the industry developed in France, Italy and Portugal. When the Turks conquered Syria and Egypt at the beginning of the 16th century the overland trade routes were closed; and trade with India virtually ceased until the 15th century when Vasco da Gama and other explorers searched for a new trade route to the East. This sea trade route between Europe and the East was monopolized by Portugal until the second half of the 16th

century when the great European trading companies began to emerge. In the 17th century, remarkable cotton textiles from the Indian subcontinent came into a market place of silk, worsteds, velvets and brocades. These hand-painted, printed and resist-dyed cottons in brilliant colours were first imported into Europe through the East India companies of England, France and the Netherlands. Their vivid colours and patterns made them highly desirable for both furnishing and fashionable clothing. From the late 17th century a cotton industry developed in Europe and, as the Industrial Revolution progressed, Lancashire in

ABOVE: *Banjara woman's skirt, from south India, decorated with squares of reverse appliqué.*

BELOW, LEFT; AND BELOW, RIGHT: *Cotton coats, worn by the Ainu of Japan, decorated in the traditional style of appliqué; small* katab chakla *with saw-toothed appliqué border designs, India.*

19

northern England became the centre of cotton manufacturing in the world, a position held until the early years of the 20th century. The enormous output was exported throughout the world, undercutting the indigenous hand-made textiles of Asia, and all but destroying the centuries-old Asian textile industry.

English cotton

R ECORDS dating from the 16th and early 17th centuries mention the so-called 'cotton' fabric in use in England, but this was very different from the cotton grown in sub-tropical regions. It was made from relatively cheap wool fleeces, unfit for the longer staple wool required for woollen fabric. Described as a woollen fabric like frieze (a coarse kind of cloth), but substantially lighter, this 'cotton' was largely manufactured in Lancashire, Westmorland and Wales. It was estimated that over 100,000 people in Wales and Shropshire made their living from making

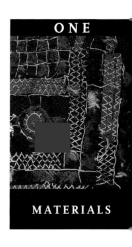

OPPOSITE, ABOVE, LEFT: *Akha girl's leggings worn to protect the legs when working in the fields, Thailand. Made of applied strips of cotton fabric.*

OPPOSITE, ABOVE, RIGHT; AND OPPOSITE BELOW (DETAIL): *Miao collar from Guizhou, China. The embroidered design is further emphasized by applied strips of cotton.*

ABOVE, RIGHT; AND BELOW, RIGHT: *Manchu woman's shoe, from China, with embroidered appliquéd designs. The stilt base is painted with white lead and contains a bell, which would jingle as she walked; intricate Hmong baby carrier in reverse appliqué, Thailand.*

these 'cottons'; between 1608 and 1609 42,000 yards of 'cotton' were recorded as being exported from Bristol. The word also refers to a finishing technique, cottoning, to set a nap upon, where a soft fluffy nap was raised and then shorn.

Cotton varieties

THERE are many different qualities of cotton, but they can be grouped mainly into long, medium and short staple. The best quality is the long staple type, which is the finest, softest and strongest. Sea Island, from the West Indies, and Egyptian cottons are included in this group and used for the finest fabrics and sewing threads. Cotton grown in the Americas is of the medium staple variety; the bulk of the world's cotton fabrics are produced from this quality type. Short staple cotton is coarser and harsher than the medium; Indian and other Asiatic cottons belong in this group. Throughout Asia, the raw, unspun cotton fibre is used as the wadding in quilted clothing and bedding.

Cotton in its raw state is almost all cellulose, with a small amount of wax. It is usually creamy white in colour, although there are some varieties that are almost brown. The raw fibre is water repellent. When purified it becomes pure white, highly absorbent and very chemically stable, which gives it a good affinity to dyes. It can be boiled or sterilized without disintegrating and is resistant to damage by alkalis. In its normal state, the fibre is not lustrous but, in 1844, John Mercer, an English textile chemist, discovered that cotton fibres will swell readily in a solution of caustic soda and, as a result, the material became stronger and dyed more readily. This chemical treatment, known

ABOVE, LEFT; ABOVE, RIGHT; BELOW LEFT; AND OPPOSITE: *Hmong apron strap in reverse appliqué, Thailand; Hmong reverse appliqué collar piece, Thailand; Korean* pojagi *sample; Kuna mola panel of reverse appliqué, Panama.*

as *mercerisation*, can produce a permanent lustre on yarns and fabric.

The versatility of the fibre is such that a very wide range of fabric structures, in light, medium and heavy weights, can be produced economically. Different treatments and processes can make cotton fabrics from a fine lawn to a heavy waterproof tent canvas, from a smooth, lustrous dress fabric to a corduroy or velvet.

WOOL AND FELT

Wool, a protein fibre produced from the fleece of sheep, is valued for its warmth. The locks of fleece are wavy (crimped) and it is this crimp that gives the wool fibre its valuable lightness and heat-retaining properties. Even a finely spun wool thread typically gives a thick, soft fabric, whether the thread is woven or knitted; these properties make most woollen fabrics unsuitable for quilting or patchwork, though wool fabric can be embellished with appliqué. The exception is lightweight or worn woollen suiting or uniform cloth, recycled into pieced quilts – a functional if heavy item, made from necessity.

Wool fleece can also be felted – when the fibres are agitated with heat, moisture and soap or alkaline solution the fibres form a firm, compressed fabric that is

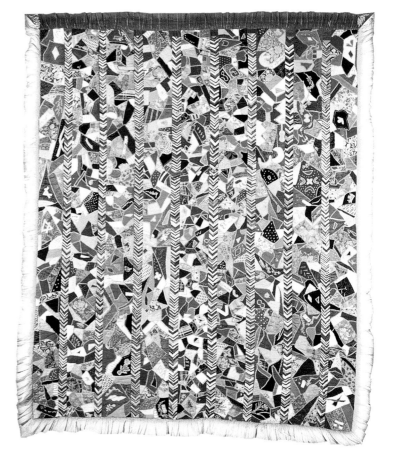

ONE

MATERIALS

OPPOSITE, TOP; OPPOSITE, LEFT; OPPOSITE, CENTRE RIGHT; AND OPPOSITE, BELOW, RIGHT: *Detail of shyrdak felt floor covering with an inlaid design of ram's horns, Central Asia; large panel of Resht work from Azerbaijan. Woven wool or felt is inlaid into a wool background and the motifs are held in place with tamboured chain stitch; 19th-century English Crazy Patchwork bed cover in silk, velvet, cotton and wool; detail of a Hungarian book cover with a wool-felt design resembling paper cut outs popular in 19th-century Europe.*

LEFT; ABOVE, RIGHT; BELOW; AND RIGHT: *Shyrdak rug, from Kirghizstan, of inlaid felt: the design is outlined with handspun wool cords; Saami reindeer herders from northern Europe wearing clothing decorated with narrow woollen braids woven on tablet looms; Peruvian gaucho with strips of fabric applied to the woollen garment; quilted felt bag from Hungary: the thickness of the fleece gives a pattern in relief, without the use of wadding.*

a very effective insulation against cold or heat. This may be a lightweight fabric, only one or two millimetres thick, or a dense, heavy, firm fabric several centimetres thick, suitable for the traditional circular tent, the *yurt* or *ger* of the nomadic peoples of Central Asia and Mongolia. Felting fleece is probably one of the oldest methods of producing a textile, originally developed perhaps by the herdsman's observation of the way in which the wool of the animal became matted. The process of turning fleece into felt is an ancient skill, as evidenced by archaeological excavations; hangings with appliquéd decoration in felt have been found in Mongolia and the Altai Mountains, dating from 400 BC. The sheep indigenous to the region have a fleece particularly suitable for making felt; the natural colour variation of the fleece is used to produce patterned felt. If brighter colours are desired, the fleece is dyed before felting. The making of felt is traditionally a woman's task, beginning with cleaning the fleece on the sheep by herding the animals through a stream. Felted fabric has no warp or weft and can be cut without

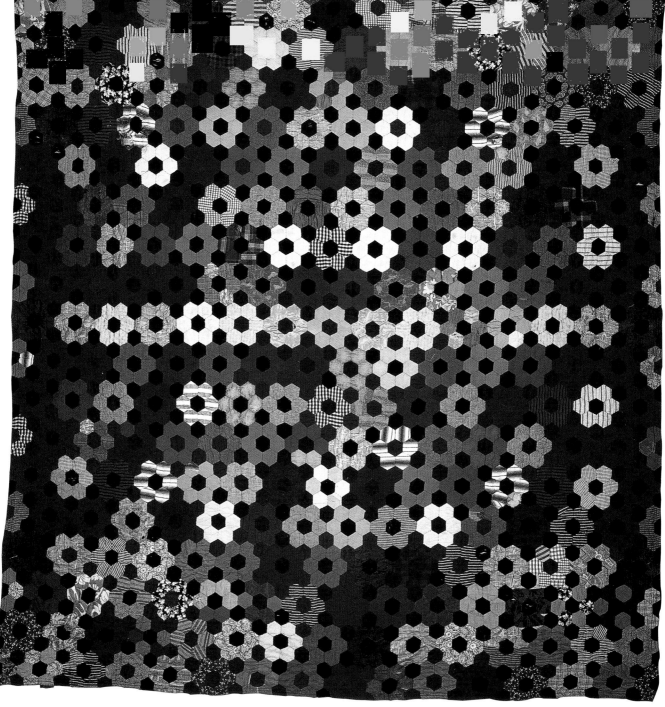

the edges fraying, making it an ideal fabric for intricate appliqué.

The uses of felt

IN Central Asia, felt is still used extensively, not only for the *yurt*, but also for large storage bags, animal trappings, floor coverings and clothing; these felted objects may be further decorated with appliqué of cotton, silk or leather, as well as embroidery, tassels, beads and coins. A method used in both Turkey and Central Asia, known as *shyrdak*, uses a counter-change technique whereby two differently coloured felts are laid one on top of the

other and a design cut with a sharp knife through both so that the pieces can then be interchanged. They can then be either laid onto a felt backing and the cut edges covered with a narrow braid, or the pieces stitched together and then outlined with two cords, one an S- and one a Z-twist cord.

A much more intricate inlay appliqué technique was used in Resht in northern Iran to make large hangings. These were made of felt, or more usually flannel, with the already complex design further embellished with embroidery.

Felt was also used for several different styles of coat or jacket throughout much of

ABOVE: *A quilt pattern of colourful hexagon rosettes often called Grandmother's Flower Garden, unusually made from wool and flannel, Wales.*

OPPOSITE, TOP: *Indigo cotton woman's jacket with applied red wool strips, typical of the tribal groups in Burma and northern Thailand.*

OPPOSITE, FAR RIGHT: *Woman's coat with a pieced skirt; indigo-dyed stitch-resist patterned wool, from Ladakh.*

OPPOSITE, BELOW, LEFT: *Making a* kepenek, *a traditional Turkish shepherd's felt cloak: working the edges and the finished design.*

Eastern Europe. The best known of these is the Hungarian *szur*, the magnificent coat of felt or skin, adorned with braiding and felt or leather appliqué. These were worn by herdsmen and other farm workers, for everyday and festive occasions, and, during the 19th century, by soldiers. Household items decorated with complex felt appliqué in the traditional *szur* colours of white and beige, or more festive red and white, are made today both for home consumption and for export.

Appliqué on felt and wool

WOOL or leather appliqué was used on wool or felt garments in the Czech Republic, Croatia, Serbia and Bosnia. In Slovakia leather appliqué was used on woollen coats. Where the decoration was red, this had a protective as well as a decorative purpose, since red was a significant colour throughout Eastern Europe. The wool clothing of the Saami, the nomadic reindeer herders of Scandinavia, is decorated with applied braids and the reindeer themselves adorned with collars of appliquéd felt.

During the 1960s Inuit women from the Canadian Northwest Territories began to make wall hangings of wool and felt, using the techniques traditionally used for clothing of hide and skin. These were made to sell, to bring much needed income into the communities that produced them, and have since become a collectable art form, expressing the traditions of the Inuit community.

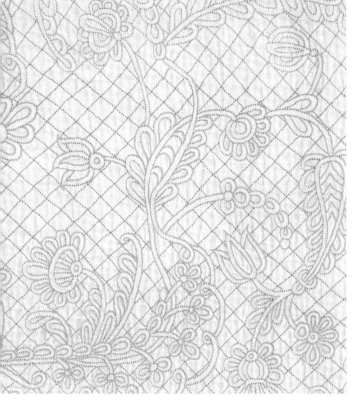

Silk

Sericulture, the breeding of silkworms to produce silk, and the use of silk have been known in China for more than 4,000 years. Tradition says that the Chinese Empress Hsi Ling Shih discovered the method of rearing silk worms and reeling off the silk filament from the cocoons – she was later deified as the Goddess of Silk. The production of silk was a closely guarded secret until it was brought to Byzantium, in the mid-6th century, by two Nestorian monks. Such was the demand for silk, both as raw fibre and as fabric, that it led to the establishment of the greatest of the trade routes – the Silk Road – which stretched from China to Italy.

Silks, dating to the 2nd century, have been found in Syria; the patterns on these silks show an Oriental influence. In Japan, silk brocades and fine silk gauze have been found that pre-date the 9th century. While

ABOVE, LEFT; AND ABOVE, RIGHT: *European cord-quilted silk coverlet, 1700; a Chinese woman wearing a wide-sleeved damask silk jacket edged with appliquéd silk ribbons.*

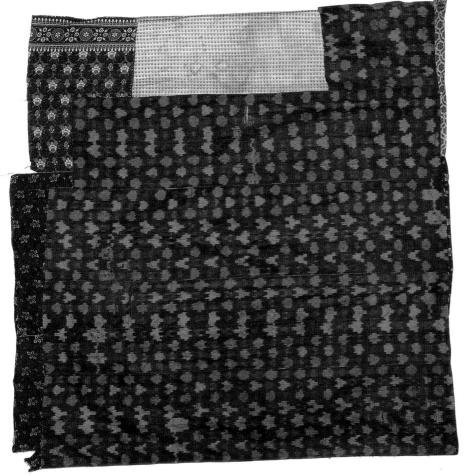

ABOVE; AND LEFT: *Silk and cotton quilted* chapan, *the universal Central Asian garment, with a lining made from different fabrics;* pardeh *(curtain) of ikat silk pieces with a printed cotton backing, from Afghanistan, early 20th century.*

OPPOSITE, BELOW LEFT; AND DETAIL: *European quilted petticoat, 1780. The detail shows petals outlined in a double row of running stitches and the flower centre filled in with a diamond pattern.*

silk was not made in ancient Europe, Rome was the market place of the West, trading in silks, fine embroideries and hangings from the Near and Far East and Egypt.

In the West, by the 14th century, Italy had become an established centre for silk weaving; then by the second half of the 17th century France succeeded Italy as the principal producer of patterned silk. Ribbons and some silks had been woven in London since the late 16th century by a predominantly Huguenot workforce, who came from France as refugees. In the

29

head of the silkworm, known as the spinneret. As the silk is spun, the two strands are stuck together by a gum called sericin which creates the protective casing known as the cocoon. When cultivated, the pupa inside the cocoon is killed to prevent the filaments from being damaged as the moth eats its way out. The wild silkworms leave one end of the cocoon open, filling it only with the gum, and making it unnecessary to kill the chrysalis inside. The cocoons are soaked in hot water to soften the sericin and the filaments from several cocoons are reeled together to

18th century raw silk for the warp travelled from Italy and China, and silk for the weft came chiefly from Persia, via Turkey; silk for the warp had to be of a higher quality since it needed to take a much greater strain than the weft. English silks were exported to Hamburg for distribution across northern Europe, Amsterdam, Copenhagen and Oslo. France exported to Central and southern Europe and to South America through Spain, where a silk-printing industry had developed. Silk fabric continued to be made throughout Asia.

From ancient times two forms of silk have been available: the first, and finest, is from the cocoon of the mulberry-feeding moth, *Bombyx mori*, and the second, known as wild silk, or tussah silk, from the cocoons of uncultivated moths, feeding on several different tree species.

Silk, the only natural filament used to create a textile, is produced by the silkworm in its larval stage. The grub is carefully looked after, feeding and resting, during which time it sheds its skin and grows a new one. After the fourth moulting it eats up to twenty times its weight in mulberry leaves and begins to make a cocoon. The silk is contained in two glands and exits through a hole in the

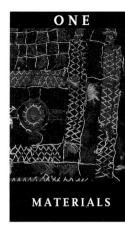

make one long, smooth thread. Only about half the silk from a cocoon can be used in filament form, the rest is cut and used to make spun silk.

China and Japan produce most of the world's cultivated silk; southern France, Italy and parts of Asia produce only small amounts. Wild silks are mainly produced in India, China and Japan, with smaller amounts being produced in Europe, the Americas and Asia. The most common type of wild silk is tussah silk, the filaments of which are coarser than the cultivated fibres, and produce fabric types such as Shantung silk, where the unevenness is a defining characteristic. The natural colour of wild silk is beige and, as bleaching can damage the silk filament, wild silk is either used in its natural colour or dyed a deeper shade.

Silk is a most remarkable and exceptionally useful textile fibre. Its long filament produces a thread that is strong and takes dye well. When two different colours are used for the warp and weft, known as 'shot' fabric, the resulting fabric appears iridescent. The quality of silk is very varied, but each type is useable, from sewing and knitting silks to heavy damasks, gauzy chiffons and silk satins, and it can be combined with other fibres

ONE

MATERIALS

RIGHT: *Silk* pojagi *wrapping cloth, from Korea, made from scraps of silk which are joined into squares until the cloth becomes the required size.*

BELOW: *English pieced narrow silk day-bed cover with silk frill, late 19th century.*

OPPOSITE, ABOVE, LEFT: *Mosaic patchwork cushion cover of dress silk and velvet, with irregular pentagon shapes, diamonds and church window patterns, England, 19th century.*

BELOW: *Moroccan woman in a velvet gown decorated with applied metallic braid and embroidery in metallic thread.*

such as cotton and linen. Blending silk with cotton not only reduces the cost, but may also make a luxurious textile more ethically acceptable: in traditional Islamic law pure silk is regarded as too indulgent a fabric, but a mixture of silk and cotton is considered permissible. This blended fabric known as *mashru* or *misru* (meaning *permitted* or *mixed*) was woven in western India, for the Arabian market.

Velvet

IT is thought that velvet was first made in Ancient China; it was known in Persia 4,000 years ago. The technique of making velvet travelled to Europe via India and the Middle East and by the Middle Ages was being made in Spain, Italy and France.

Richly woven silk brocades and velvets were prized and coveted fabrics in the Middle Ages and Renaissance Europe, although always the province of the wealthy classes and the Church. Expensive fabrics, and the garments made from them, were depicted in careful detail in the European potraiture of the time. Gifts of costly fabric and clothing were given to favoured persons throughout the known world.

The textile structure of the fabric is a compound weave, where a supplementary pile warp is interlaced with the ground warp, but wire is inserted under the pile warp and loops or floats are thus produced. As the wire is withdrawn, the loops are cut and the pile is formed. It can also be made as a double fabric with the pile in the middle section – as the pile is cut, two fabrics are produced, face to face. Patterns can be created within the velvet by having certain areas cut and others uncut; this is

known as figured velvet. The backing fabric and the supplementary yarn can be silk, rayon, synthetics or cotton – each will give a different look to the finished fabric; the lighter the pile, the softer the velvet. Silk velvet is the most luxurious and softest of all velvets and cotton is the least supple and most stable, best used in upholstery or curtains. Synthetic velvets are often used for ease of care.

A velveteen fabric is made up of a ground weave and a large number of weft floats, which are cut and brushed after the fabric has been woven, to create the pile. As the pile of velveteen is not, at the weaving stage, as dense as that of velvet, it is cheaper to produce, though not as durable, and was a favourite choice for children's clothing in 19th-century Europe and North America.

In France, Italy and Spain in the Middle Ages appliqué work could be found on furnishings and saddle trappings, sometimes of leather and sometimes of velvet or heavy brocade which was stiffened. Since both velvet and silk are

Left: *Crazy patchwork of silks and velvets from Ontario, Canada, c. 1910.*

Above, right: *'Bow tie' block patchwork quilt in velvet, Ontario, Canada, early 20th century.*

Below, left: *Appliquéd velvet cushion, from Palestine, with embroidery in metallic thread.*

too costly to waste, even the small pieces are used in appliqué and patchwork. Patchwork cloths from Central Asia use scraps of brilliantly coloured ikat silk and velvet among the more utilitarian cotton fabrics. Ikat velvet is perhaps the most complex and luxurious silk velvet fabric of all. As the production of velvet became mechanized during the Industrial Revolution in Europe it became more readily available, especially as the cheaper velveteen. Velvet is frequently to be found in the Log Cabin quilts and crazy patchwork quilts of the late 19th century, both in Europe and North America.

33

LEATHER AND SKIN

LEATHER IS the skin of an animal, bird, reptile or fish, which has been cured to render it supple and durable. In order to cure the leather it has to go through a process known as tanning. Various methods of tanning and curing were developed in different societies – for instance, some tribal groups in North America used the brains of the dead animal to produce a wonderfully soft, supple skin.

In Prehistoric times the only form of tanning was that known as tawing, where the dressed article was returned to the condition of a raw hide by immersion in water. The word tanning is derived from the process of vegetable tanning; the tannin from different tree barks were used to prepare the skins. Skins and hides were layered in a pit with bark and water, the mixture changed every few months, using various strengths of the infusion. Today, tannic acid comes from plants instead of bark. The finished colour of the vegetable-tanned leathers ranges from pale cream to reddish brown.

Dyeing leather

THE mineral tanning of leather, using alum, together with salt, produced a stiff, pure white leather, examples of which have been found in Ancient Egypt. Among Ancient Egyptians and Phoenicians, the dyeing of alum-tanned leather required a high degree of skill; a piece of vivid red stained leather, over 4,000 years old, has been found in an Egyptian tomb. Coloured leather was expensive and was therefore worn to display rank and wealth. Black was formed from tannins mixed with iron and copper salts. Vivid colours were produced on tawed leather by mixing aluminium salts with vegetable dyes. Since the end of the 19th century many new methods of both tanning and finishing leather have been

ABOVE, LEFT; AND ABOVE, RIGHT: *Here intricate leather appliqué has been chosen to create a border design. Gold-covered goatskin has been cut into a lattice-like design and backed with coloured fabrics, from Indonesia, used to decorate ceremonial objects. White beads (above) add extra embellishment.*

LEFT: *Cutting camel leather appliqué, in Gujarat, north-western India. In India leather work is considered to be a low-caste occupation.*

OPPOSITE, FAR RIGHT: *North Pakistani leather slip-on shoes with appliqué designs of self-coloured leather.*

TOP LEFT; TOP CENTRE; AND TOP RIGHT:
*Different-coloured backing fabrics show through
the lattice of gold-covered leather of this Indonesian
piece; Algerian Tuareg bag of leather with leather
appliqué and large leather tassels. The bag is lined
with printed cotton; detail of a man's sleeveless
jacket of leather appliqué backed with thick wool
cloth, from the Nasaud region in Transylvania.*

ABOVE, LEFT: *Inuit family wearing skin clothing
decorated with applied braid; different-coloured
furs were also used in appliqué.*

introduced; chromium salts were first
used to produce a leather that was highly
resistant to water.

Patchwork and appliqué

Fur, skin and leather have been used in
a range of patchwork and appliquéd
items, the advantages of no directional
weave and non-fraying edges making
the advantages of hide and skin similar to
those of felt. The sub-Arctic peoples of
Northern America and Siberia used fish
skin, particularly salmon skin, to make
clothing and bags. Fish skin makes a light,
strong material, quite unlike the slippery
skin associated with the freshly killed fish.
Australia's indigenous peoples produced
patched skin rugs, which were traded with
the first European explorers in the early
18th century. Similarly, in Peru today,
llama skin rugs or blankets are made to
sell to tourists. Since the 19th century, if
not before, Russian and Eastern European
folk dress has featured patchwork and
appliqué in cloth, fur and leather, and the
inhabitants of the Russian Arctic make full
use of a variety of hides for their clothing –

boots and robes are appliquéd with braids.
In North-Eastern China there are two sub
groups of formerly nomadic peoples, the
Oraqen and Ewenki, whose men wear hide
jackets and coats of wolfskin, decorated
with black hide appliquéd patches. In
some cultures, working with animal skin is
considered 'unclean' and is the traditional
occupation of a lower or separate caste.

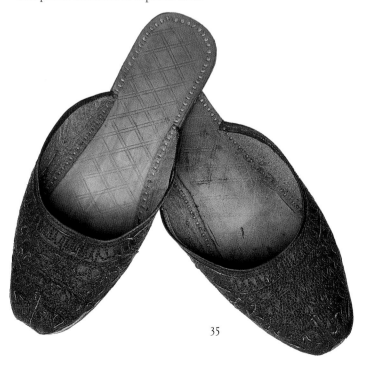

PLANT FIBRES

BARK-FIBRE CLOTH was used extensively in North-west America, in ancient Central America as far south as the Andes and Amazon, in Central Africa and the tropical areas of the Pacific Ocean. The fabric was obtained by soaking the bark of certain trees, including mulberry, the bread fruit tree, the fig tree and the hibiscus bush, in water and then beating it until the resultant cloth was very thin and pliable. The cloth was then decorated with a painted resist or printed patterns and made into ordinary clothing or ceremonial hangings and garments. Bark-fibre cloth is also known as wood-bast fabric or tapa cloth.

Hemp, jute, ramie and nettle

HEMP, jute, ramie and nettle fibres all come from the stalks of plants, the various soft ingredients of which are made strong by cellulose fibres. As with flax, the plants need to decompose, leaving behind the fibres (a process known as 'retting' in the manufacture of linen) and they then need to be subject to a combined beating and combing which straightens the fibres and removes any impurities. The resulting fibre can be spun.

Hemp is grown in most European countries, Asia, Africa and North America and was used in both rope and textile manufacture; fabrics have been found in Egyptian, Roman and Coptic burials. It is still valuable for the manufacture of cord, rope and string. As hemp uses less water when growing and in production and can be successfully grown without agricultural chemicals there is an increasing interest in growing it as a commercial fibre. Jute plants grow in hot, damp areas, mainly in Pakistan, Bangladesh, India and China. Other countries took up the spinning and weaving of jute, which is not as durable as hemp, and it was used mainly for sacks, mats and wrapping cloths. Ramie, a native of China and the East Indies, comes from a species of nettle; other nettle fibres have also been used and fragments of fibre from the nettle have been found in late Bronze Age urns from Denmark. Fabrics woven from nettle fibre found their way into Central European folklore – the story of seven brothers, turned by a malevolent witch into swans whose spell is broken by clothing the brothers in shirts made of nettle fibre, is typical.

Japanese plant fibres

IN Japan, before the arrival of cotton, the common people were clothed in whatever material was available to them – nettle, ramie, hemp, mulberry or linden bark. Most of these bast fibres grew wild and harvesting and processing were difficult. For warmth – plants fibres do not provide warmth in the same way as wool or silk, for instance – clothing was layered, one garment on top of another. The hemp fibres were thin and offered little protection from the cold, but stitching several layers together created a warmer material, with the stitching running parallel to the warp and weft to pack the fibres together, making them less

TOP LEFT; LEFT; OPPOSITE, TOP; OPPOSITE, CENTRE; AND OPPOSITE, ABOVE, RIGHT: Kuba cloth made from raphia fibre; bark cloth patchwork dance skirt with an embroidered raphia edging; patchwork Kuba raphia skirt with alternating stitch-resist squares; Kuba raphia skirt with rectangular patchwork pieces, embroidered in raphia fibre and with stitch-resist borders; Kuba raphia skirt with geometric appliqué designs, all from the Democratic Republic of the Congo.

ABOVE, RIGHT; AND OPPOSITE, BELOW, RIGHT: Ainu people in elm bark fibre coats with geometric appliqué designs; Ainu woman's coat of elm bark fibre, Hokkaido, both from Japan.

OPPOSITE, BELOW, LEFT: Tongan women wearing bark cloth with painted geometric patterns.

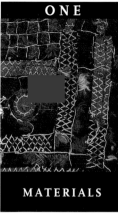

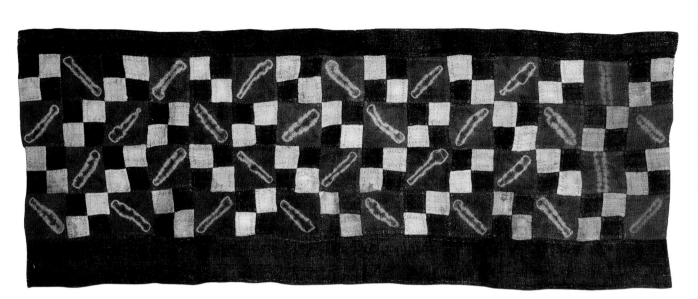

pervious to wind and rain. This was the beginning of *sashiko* quilting.

Raphia

RAPHIA, or raffia, is extracted from the leaves of a palm tree grown in Central and West Africa, and on the island of Madagascar. In Europe and North America it is used for garden twine, but in the Democratic Republic of the Congo it is a luxurious textile, worn as dance skirts. The raphia is spun and woven and then, as with bark cloth, it must be soaked and beaten to soften the cloth, which results in small worn places on the finished fabric. This was the origin of the appliquéd Kuba cloths – the appliqué patches, originally added to cover the thin areas, are now a deliberate decorative element.

SYNTHETICS

Fibres are usually categorized into three types: cellulose, protein and synthetic. Cellulose (natural, rayon, acetate) and protein fibres (wool and silk) consist of polymers from vegetable or animal growth. Synthetic fibres are manufactured by adding together many molecules to create a large molecule; a process known as polymerization. These polymers have been synthesized from petroleum and coal-tar products.

Rayon

Natural fibres still remain the principal source of the world's textiles, but the ever-present need to reduce costs and simplify processes has led to experiments to produce synthetic fibres. The first man-made fibres were developed from attempts to make artificial

Right: *Child's quilted dressing gown of synthetic fabric and wadding, England, 1960s.*

Below: Chakla *from Gujarat, north-western India; the older, heavily beaded centre panel is surrounded by pieced borders of shiny synthetic fabric.*

Opposite, above: *Detail of an English quilt made from printed polycotton and knitted nylon fabrics. Its value is functional rather than aesthetic.*

Opposite, below: *Indian book cover constructed from squares and rectangles of man-made silk with embroidery.*

silk in the late 1880s. This fibre was eventually allowed to develop as a textile in its own right, instead of being thought of as a substitute for silk; it was re-named rayon.

Regenerated man-made fibres, which include rayon, acetate and triacetate fibres, are all of a cellulose type, chemically similar to vegetable fibres. The process starts with timber, usually spruce or eucalyptus. It is almost impossible to make vegetable protein fibres that are chemically similar to animal fibres and are strong enough for normal use, but these fibres can be used with other fibres.

Commercial production

Synthetic man-made fibres, such as the earliest types of nylon or polyamide, were in commercial production in the late 1930s. Polyesters, such as Dacron and Terylene, were

discovered in 1941; the first commercial production of acrylics, such as Courtelle and Dralon, came in 1950, followed by elastomerics, such as Lycra.

Yarns are produced by twisting together long, thin fibres as in a spun yarn, or a continuous filament yarn. Continuous filament yarns are made by extruding long, unbroken threads and adding a twist to hold them together. Synthetic fibres are produced in this way, extruding fibre-forming substances, in liquid form, through the fine holes of a spinneret. The liquid hardens and can be stretched and twisted to form a yarn. Smooth fabrics, such as satins and taffetas, are woven from continuous filament yarns. In the production of man-made fibres the filaments may be collected together into a thick rope and cut up into short lengths to form staple fibre, which can then be spun. When first developed, the continuous filament yarn did not compete effectively with spun yarns but, since the 1950s, yarn bulking and texturing has altered the drape and handle of such fabrics and extended their use.

With the new textile forms came the need to re-think how to dye these fibres; many continuous filament yarns must be coloured while still a liquid, before extrusion. Parts of the yarn could be treated to accept a dye and other parts to repel the same dye. Using a mix of

different fibres, the range of design possibilities is infinite, added to which is the use of computer technology to determine patterns and colour. Of all the synthetic fabrics, nylon and polyester cotton are the most used for patchwork and appliqué techniques, probably because of their similarity to the older traditional fabrics. While these new fabrics have the advantage of cheapness and colour fastness, they have the disadvantage of being difficult to work with.

RIBBON AND BRAID

Rᴵʙʙᴏɴꜱ ᴀɴᴅ braids are frequently used as a decorative feature of clothing; when applied to a plain cloth, they can resemble a woven or embroidered finish. Many diverse groups of people have created very distinctive clothing with braid as the main decorative element. There is some similarity in the clothing and culture of the various peoples of the Arctic and Sub-Arctic regions of Europe, Russia and North America. The Saami are a reindeer-herding people who live in northern Europe. They weave narrow braids on tablet looms, which are then appliquéd to their traditional clothing. Their clothing is generally in a shade of blue with a predominantly red trim; white, green and yellow are often used alongside the red as accent colours. The braid is applied in lines, following the construction lines of the garment. As well as decorating their clothing, bright, plain-coloured strips of woollen cloth are applied to a background of wool, frequently dyed indigo, to make wall hangings.

Geographical variations

Tʜᴇ Greenlanders today are of mixed Inuit and European descent. In the southern part of their region they raise sheep and hunt seal, arctic fox and polar bear. Winter clothing is generally made from woollen felt or skins; their summer tunics are of heavy cotton, imported from Venezuela. The tunics are knee length at the front and slightly longer at the back, with waist-high slits decorated with bands of bright-coloured, plain cotton fabric, applied to the background fabric; these are sometimes embroidered.

In the Russian Arctic, the inhabitants make full use of a variety of hides for their clothing, and both the boots and their robes are decorated with applied braids.

In Eastern Europe waistcoats often feature as part of a traditional form of dress, rarely worn for everyday wear, but kept for special occasions. The men's

ᴀʙᴏᴠᴇ: *Bosnian woman wearing a garment with large elaborate sleeves edged with applied ribbon and braid. Metallic braids were a favourite decoration on both men and women's clothing.*

Lᴇꜰᴛ: *Man's woollen coat, from Syria, with appliquéd braid.*

Bᴇʟᴏᴡ: *Stitching an appliqué border, Gujarat, north-western India.*

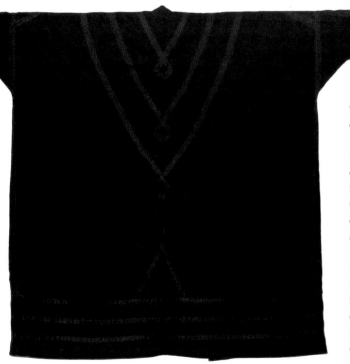

waistcoats, in particular, are frequently decorated with braiding.

Throughout North Africa and the Middle East braids are used in multiple rows to decorate garments, the decoration usually following the openings of the garment. Gold or gold-coloured braid is often used on velvet, especially on waistcoats for boys and men, in Pakistan and Afghanistan.

In South-west China the women of the Miao hill tribe create panels to decorate the collars, cuffs, shoulders and lapels of festive courting jackets, using silk braids couched down on the cloth. Folded and pleated ribbons also create border designs on clothing.

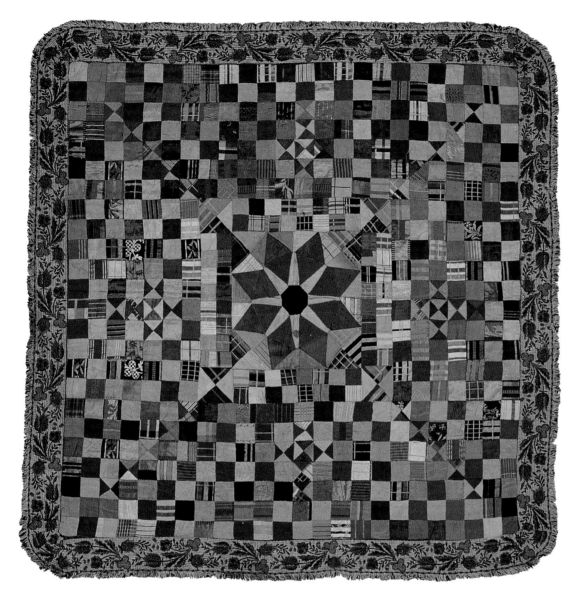

Ribbonwork

IN the early 18th century ribbonwork, the art of cutting and sewing silk ribbons onto trade cloth for decoration, was introduced to the Native Americans. The development of the technique was entirely dependent upon the introduction of trade goods, but the uses and designs are completely indigenous. Silk ribbons were first presented as gifts to the Native Americans and the early ribbons were narrow, but later ribbons reached widths of three to four inches (8 to 10 cm). In its simplest form, a design is cut into one ribbon and it is hand sewn onto another, differently coloured ribbon. The panel is then stitched to the fabric of a garment, often leggings or a shawl. Colour preference was given to those with symbolic meaning. Many contemporary examples of ribbonwork shirts and skirts are made especially

to accompany the dead, the cut ribbon symbolizing the whole being split – half in this world and half in the spirit world. The ribbonwork produced by the Great Lakes tribes combines Native American artistry with non-Native American textiles and still continues today as an art form.

The inclusion of ribbons was important for the more luxurious versions of Log Cabin patchwork and it coincided with the increased use of the domestic sewing machine. In 1886 *Weldon's Practical Patchwork* gave instructions for 'Ribbon Patchwork' – with strips sewn over papers in the traditional English manner.

ABOVE: *Nineteenth-century English patchwork table cover made from 'Coventry' silk ribbons; the border is constructed from cotton and silk furnishing braid.*

ABOVE, RIGHT; AND BELOW: *Chinese woman wearing a coat with applied ribbon and braid edging; modern Lahu woman's skirt of interlaced designs in narrow strips of polyester cotton appliquéd onto plain fabric, northern Thailand.*

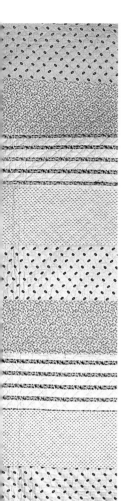

PRINTED TEXTILES

BASIC PATTERNING techniques have been used for ornamentation for thousands of years as far back as 20000 BC. Tribal peoples in central South America and Borneo still paint images on their skins and, for centuries, plant dyes such as henna have been used to create designs to beautify the body.

Block printing

IT is thought that printing blocks were used in India as far back as 3000 BC and by the time Alexander the Great invaded India in 327 BC brightly coloured painted and printed fabrics and tied and dyed cottons were already an established means of decorating cloth. The setting up of new trade routes followed and the patterned fabrics of India·spread by land and sea to Asia, Egypt, North Africa and the Greek and Roman ports. Many Greek and Roman writers of the time of Christ refer to the coastal trade in patterned cottons. In the 2nd century AD Arab traders brought Indian fabrics into Europe and the trade routes were extended into Central and West Africa. During this same period block printing is thought to have been carried out in China and during the 3rd and 4th centuries resist and stencilling techniques were introduced into Japan, by the Chinese.

In a grave in Upper Egypt, a complete child's tunic, dating from the 4th century AD, has been found. Made of white linen and printed in blue, the making up of the

LEFT; ABOVE, RIGHT; AND BELOW, LEFT: *Printed cotton fabrics, 19th century, England; Indian hand-carved wooden printing blocks (top row and left), Indonesian metal tjap (below, right) and stamps carved from calabash for printing adinkra cloth in Ghana (below, centre); detail of an English patchwork quilt of printed cotton fabrics.*

garment shows that it came from a length of printed fabric. A wooden printing block, of the same period, was also found. The earliest two-colour print, from the 6th century, was found on the same site. Other printed textiles have been discovered in Persia (from the 6th and 7th centuries), Peru and ancient Mexico.

In Europe the first known example of early textile printing also dates from the 6th century. Documentary evidence mentions block printing in Italy in the 13th century, but it is not possible to trace any continuous development of this technique. There is no evidence of a cloth printers' guild in the Middle Ages and the names of cloth printers do not appear in

any records until around 1500, when they are noted as also printing books. The craft seems to have developed from the desire to produce cheap imitations of rare and expensive textiles. A document from Nuremberg in Germany, dating from 1450, gives instructions on how to copy animals and flowers from cloth of gold, the magnificent brocades from the Orient and Italy.

Trade with India

IN 1592 an English privateer brought a Spanish ship with its cargo of calicoes, lawns, quilts, carpets and other luxury goods into Devonport. The rich colours of the dyes and the skilled designs of the printed and painted cloths persuaded English merchants to form the East India Company in 1601 and establish direct communications with India. A Dutch company followed in 1602 and a French company in 1664. Attempts were made to produce imitations of the Indian prints and calicos; the first English calico printing factory was set up in 1690.

European import restrictions and the mechanization of roller printing in the 18th century caused a reversal of fortunes and Indian markets were flooded with very cheap so-called 'Manchester' prints from England, which all but destroyed the traditional printed textile industry in India. However, with the introduction of modern machinery and reactive dyestuffs after World War II, a resurgence of printed textiles took place in some areas of India. And today, with the current interest in ethical and ecological processes, small-scale hand-block printing using natural dyes is undergoing something of a revival and finds a ready sale in the West.

ONE

MATERIALS

LEFT: *Hexagon rosettes showing a range of printed cotton dress fabrics, 20th century, England.*

RIGHT: *Detail of samples of printed cottons, early 20th century, England.*

BELOW; AND BELOW, INSET: *Simple quilt made using printed cottons from a sample book, early 20th century, England; hand-block printing cloth, Gujarat, north-western India.*

OPPOSITE, BELOW, RIGHT: *Hawaiian woman in a block-printed cotton skirt.*

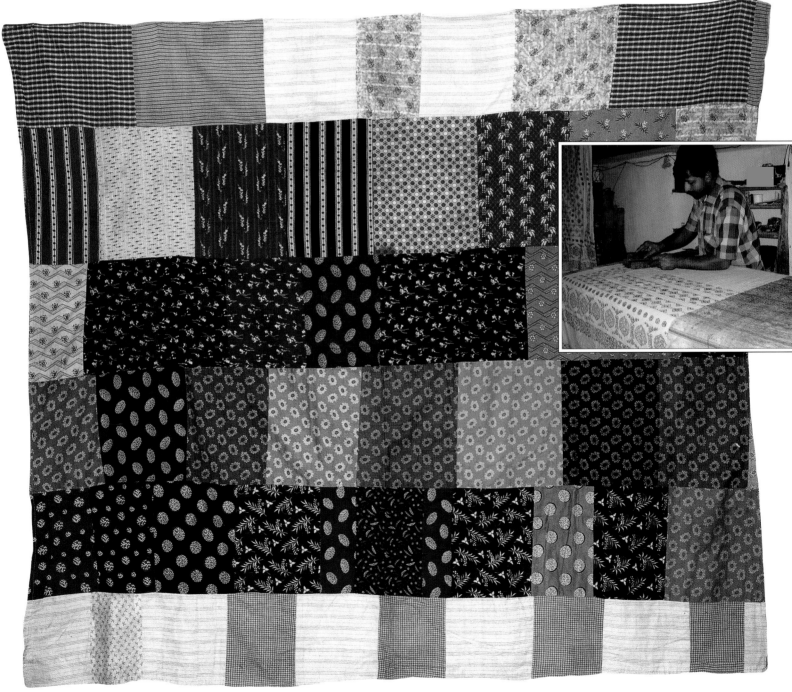

DYEING

THE ART of dyeing and creating patterns with dyes was carried out, in ancient times, in China, India and Persia. Phoenician traders are thought to have brought these skills to Egypt where some of the earliest traces of dyed and patterned textiles have been found. Thousands of examples of dyed and undyed fabrics have been discovered in Egyptian burial grounds, so well preserved in the sandy soils that the colours have remained strong. The Phoenician and Alexandrian merchants exported dyestuff to Greece and other parts of the then known world. Knowledge of how to dye textiles spread to Europe via Italy. Woad was used in Europe from 2500 BC until 800 BC; it is thought that other dyes used in prehistoric Europe included a blue from dwarf elder, red from madder, yellow from weld, purple from bilberry or whortleberry and black which sometimes came from oak galls. Historically, primitive peoples usually made the fabric first and then dyed and patterned it later, whereas more sophisticated societies tended to dye the yarn before weaving the fabric.

Techniques

THE first attempts at colouring led to substances that were both water soluble and direct; the simplest of dyeing methods is to boil up the dye material in water and place the yarn or textile into the solution. Of these direct or substantive dyes, lichens are the most important. With the discovery that colours became permanent with the addition of a mordant, which helps the dye cling onto the textile, techniques progressed rapidly. These adjective dyes require different mordants, the most common, of mineral origin,

LEFT; AND BELOW: *Dyeing yarn with madder, Turkey; South African hand and machine-stitched, resist-patterned indigo-dyed cloth which was folded before stitching to create symmetrical patterns. Also a starch-resist indigo cloth from the Czech Republic.*

Natural dyes

NATURAL dyes from various plant, animal or mineral sources were the only ones available until synthetic dyes were discovered in the mid-19th century. One of the oldest animal dyes was the 'Tyrian Purple', extracted from shellfish and used by the Phoenicians. Bright red dyes came from the dried bodies of the cochineal beetle; vegetable dyes from young and vigorous plants (all parts of the plants are used). Dyes can also be extracted from the heartwood of trees and minerals can be used. Iron rust, for example, dyes a deep red, which can be seen in the sails of boats in the Mediterranean.

being alum, tin, chrome and iron. In the 1850s, as a result of scientific work to provide substitutes or alternatives to natural products, the first reliable alternative to a natural dye was mauveine, from coal tar, developed by a British chemist, William Perkin. At around the same time a synthetic mordant was developed by Friedrich Wöhler, a German chemist, which could be used to stabilize the dye colours. These aniline dyes became available in brilliant colours which, along with their colourfastness and ease of use, made them popular worldwide and, in many places, the use of natural dyes was virtually forgotten.

Indigo

INDIGO has long been regarded as the most important of all dyestuffs. It is the only plant dye that is colourfast and will dye both animal and vegetable fibres.

ABOVE, LEFT: *Japanese* kotatsu, *table cover. The cloth is patched and repatched, using indigo-dyed cotton cloth and* kasuri *(ikat cloth).*

TOP RIGHT; AND ABOVE, RIGHT: *Dye vat and raw fleece prior to dyeing; fibres dyed with madder, indigo and weld drying, both Turkey.*

OPPOSITE, ABOVE, RIGHT: *Han Chinese indigo 'socks' with quilted sole and stitched heel.*

It has been obtained from a wide variety of plants: *Indigofera tinctoria*, native to India and China; *Indigofera suffruticosa* from South and Central America; *Lonchocarpus cyanescens* from West Africa; *Isatis tinctoria*, more commonly known as woad, native to the Middle East; and *Polygonum tinctorium*, known as Dyer's knotweed. *Indigofera* means 'indigo-bearing' and the species name *tinctoria* or *tinctorium* means

'used in dyeing'. The process of indigo vat dyeing is fascinating – the yellow-dyed yarn or fabric turns through green to blue as it is lifted out of the vat and exposed to the oxygen in the air. Fabrics dyed with indigo range in colour from light, milky blue to deep purple bronzes.

Cloth dyed with indigo has been found in Ancient Egyptian tombs, dating from 2500 BC. It is thought that indigo dye technology travelled to Japan from China before the 7th century and fragments of cloth and garments, showing the tradition of indigo dyeing, were excavated between 1964 and 1971 in Mali, West Africa, the oldest garments dating from the 11th century. In Medieval Europe, woad, which grew easily, was used to satisfy the growing demand among the ordinary people for blue cloth. It was not until the 16th century that *Indigofera tinctoria* was introduced into Europe from India. The use of indigo

was gladly accepted in Britain and the Netherlands, but was resisted in France and Germany, where there were large woad-growing industries. Importing indigo became a major activity for both the Dutch East India Company and the British East India Company, founded in the early 1600s. The first synthetic indigo dye was introduced in the late 19th century and, because of its constant colour, largely replaced natural indigo.

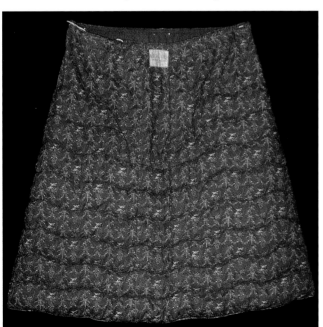

In West Africa and South-East Asia indigo blue is still the most popular colour of all the dyes. The Tuareg of the Sahara regard skin 'blued' by this cloth, which is wound around the head and face, as a mark of prestige.

Indigo is still used to dye denim jeans, the modern equivalent of the working man's clothes and, in some areas of the world, the belief that indigo repels snakes and insects has helped to preserve its use by agricultural workers.

Red

RED, the colour of blood, was one of man's earliest and most significant colours used to dye fibres and cloth. True scarlet dye from the dried bodies of the Kermes insect was found in textile fibres, dating from 1727 BC, on a Neolithic site in France. It was believed to be more permanent than cochineal and brighter than madder. There is evidence that red dye from the cochineal beetle was used by the Assyrians before the 7th century BC; madder (*Rubia tinctorum*) made from the dried and ground-up roots of a plant found in Asia was used in Ancient Egypt and the classical world to produce many shades of

red. It was said to be indispensable for dyeing woollens and leather. In England, large deposits of madder composts have been found in York, the throw outs of a Viking dyer. Commercial crops of madder were grown in England in the 11th and 12th centuries, but most madder was imported.

Turkey Red is the name given to the most brilliant of all scarlet dyes made from madder; it is one of the most permanent dyes known. The process to produce the dye was developed in the Near East and, before western European dyers had mastered the technique, cotton yarn was sent to the Levant to be dyed and then re-imported. In the second half of the 18th

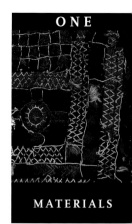

ONE

MATERIALS

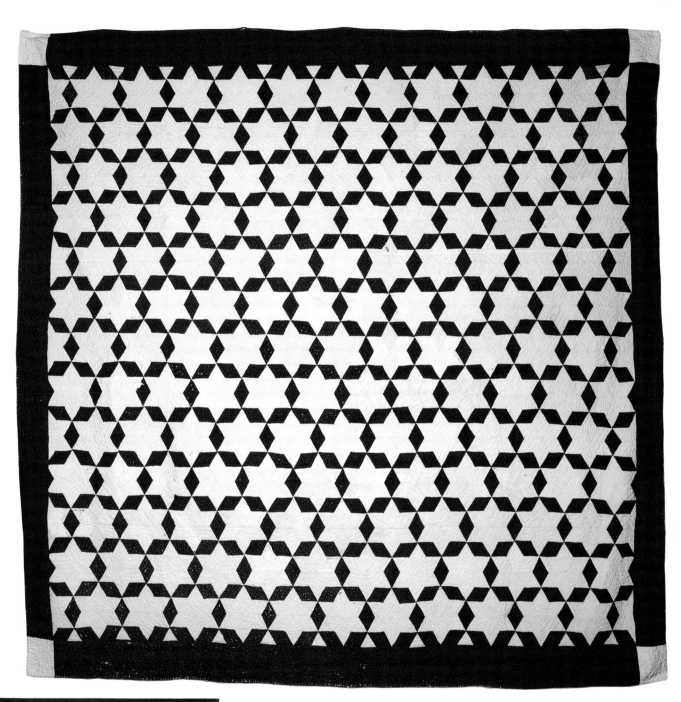

century the French were the first to attempt to dye Turkey Red and in the 1780s the knowledge of how to produce it reached Britain with a series of French dyers. By 1790 there were successful dyeworks for dyeing yarn in Scotland and England.

The process to produce Turkey Red was complicated, but once made, it was used to dye cloth in enormous quantities. At the height of its popularity, Turkey Red fabrics were found around the world: for the bandannas worn in India, by cowboys in North America and by British sailors. By 1900 synthetic red dyes that matched the colour in its brilliance had been developed and the madder-based dye was in decline.

The dyeing of blues and reds were the preserve of the 'great dyers', where high degrees of skill and knowledge were needed. They show us the best of the dyed textiles.

USES

FAR LEFT; ABOVE, LEFT; ABOVE, RIGHT;
LEFT; AND BELOW: *Kuna mola design,
San Blas Islands of Panama; English cotton
patchwork skirt, c. 1960–70; child's hat made
by the Lisu of Thailand; Turkish patchwork
mihrab; 19th-century cotton patchwork quilt
from Sind, Pakistan.*

INTRODUCTION

THE THREE related techniques of quilting, patchwork and appliqué have been employed for such an astonishingly diverse range of uses, sometimes out of necessity or sometimes as a conspicuous display of wealth.

HOUSEHOLD

A HOUSEHOLD, be it settled or nomadic, has always needed textiles to increase the comfort of the occupants. In the poorest of households bedding and floor coverings may be made from patched and pieced cloths, possibly padded with extra layers of cloth or wadding, but even the humblest of objects can easily be decorated with the necessary stitching and patching. For example, Banjara storage bags, or the *kanthas* of Bangladesh, or the *boro* textiles from Japan are stitched through many layers and began as utilitarian objects but are now as decorative as they are functional. Other household textiles such as curtains, wall hangings, cushions and the decorative trappings for animals serve a functional purpose, but also display deliberate ornamentation, sometimes in order to enhance the status of the owner or sometimes to celebrate a significant event. Some household textiles and animal trappings also serve a symbolic or protective function; for instance, an animal's tasselled, beaded and appliquéd harness not only indicates the importance of the animal and owner, but is also thought to protect the animal from the evil eye, disease or misfortune.

ABOVE, RIGHT: *Indigo-dyed girl's hood made by the Akha tribe of northern Thailand with rows of saw-toothed appliqué typical of the tribe.*

ABOVE, LEFT: *Crazy patchwork bed cover of printed dress and furnishing cottons dating from the 1940s to the 1960s, England.*

LEFT: *Linen and silk bed valance with an appliqué design couched with cord, 17th century.*

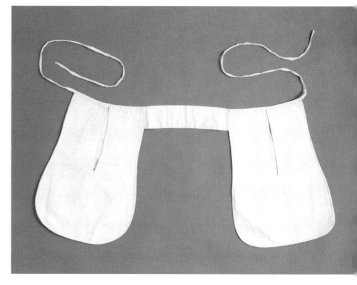

CLOTHING

CLOTHING MAY in its most basic form simply provide protection and warmth, but it almost always displays information about the wearer's status and cultural origin. What was once a necessary and practical solution to the problem of how to extend the life of a garment or how to use every scrap of fabric has become a vehicle for ornamentation and a display of skill and artistry. Clothing, perhaps more than any other object, is used to show status, sometimes on one special day such as the elaborate dress of the bride or the outfit of a child taking first communion; or a symbol of a chosen life path – the uniform, with its symbols of rank and affiliation or the monk or religious mendicant. In many cultures clothing may convey detailed information about the social status of the wearer such as their caste, occupation or marital status, or may give clues as to their village or region. Babies and small children, vulnerable and precious, are often given items of clothing that will protect them from misfortune or confuse the evil eye. Thus, young boys are given a hat in the shape of a fierce animal to frighten away malevolent spirits, or a much loved child will be dressed in symbolically ragged clothing to fool the spirits into believing the child to be worthless and beneath their notice.

ABOVE, LEFT: *Cantonese family wearing garments with applied ribbon and braid. The maid is wearing much plainer clothing, 19th century.*

ABOVE, RIGHT: *Marseilles quilted pockets. They were tied around the waist underneath a skirt with access via slits in the side seams of the top garment, 18th century.*

BELOW, LEFT: *Ibibio man's masquerade costume, West Africa. The complex patterns are made of narrow strips of cloth.*

RITUAL

BOTH DRESS and purpose-made cloths have often formed an important part of rites of passage and other rituals. Birth, naming ceremonies, circumcision, puberty rituals, marriage and death have all required cloths or significant items of dress as part of the rite. Textiles also are given in offering at shrines and temples, both as gifts and to decorate the church, temple or shrine. Smaller versions of such cloths may be sold to pilgrims to take home, to decorate their own household shrine or as a memento of the pilgrimage. Decorated cloths are used in the household shrine or shrine corner in many parts of the world, as a way of marking out the space as separate, devoted to the deity.

There seems no end to the infinite variety of stitched and decorated textiles used for all aspects of life in almost every part of the world. Humble and functional, or opulent and ornate, they speak of labour, skill, necessity and love.

HOUSEHOLD

Bedding and
seating
Floor and wall
coverings
Bags and storage
Ephemera
Recycled

BELOW: *The mid-19th century was the heyday of the appliquéd quilt in North America; this style is reminiscent of the Baltimore quilts.*

OPPOSITE, ABOVE: *The patchwork basket block has long been a favourite in North America. Here it is shown with appliquéd flowers, 20th century.*

OPPOSITE, BELOW, LEFT; AND BELOW, RIGHT (DETAIL): *American patchwork quilt, dating from the Civil War (1861–65); detail of a variation of a four-patch block known as the Lily of the Field.*

Bedding

THERE are many words for bedding in the English language; twilt or hap, known in rural North America and the north of England, eiderdown or comforter, coverlet, counter-pane or bedspread and quilt. In Europe the term 'quilt' is very often also used to describe an eiderdown or comforter, a very different object from a traditional quilt. An eiderdown, like a duvet, is essentially a bag with internal divisions or pockets – these internal pockets are filled with a warmth-entrapping filling such as feathers or down, or, often today, synthetic

TWO

HOUSEHOLD

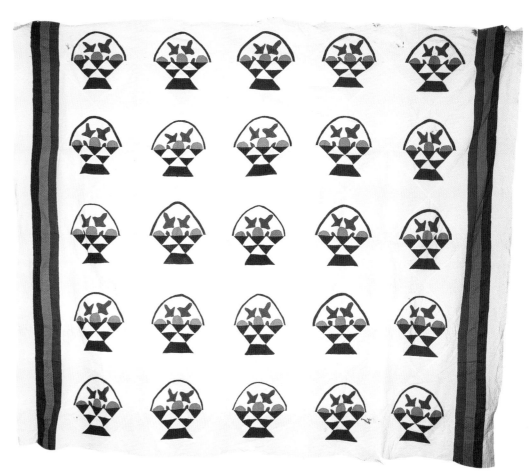

fibre. A quilt, by comparison, is much flatter and has a front and back layer with a middle layer of wadding, which may be an old blanket, cotton fibre, old wool, cotton or flannelette fabric. Bed coverings may also be referred to as counterpane, thought to have derived from the French word contrepoint, meaning backstitch – the stitch once used in quilting – or coverlet, possibly an Anglicization of couvrelit (bed cover). The *tivaivai* of Polynesia are unwadded and unquilted bed covers distinguished by large, usually floral appliqué designs.

The origin of many European quilts can be determined by the motifs and pattern used for the quilting. The best-known and most easily recognized regional styles are the English North Country, the Welsh and the Amish, which was a blend of both the

former. Padded motifs and corded quilting as well as plain quilting were used for bed quilts in France and Italy. During the 19th century the bed quilt went out of use in most parts of Europe and factory-made bed covers became a cheaper alternative. One such cover was the Marcella quilt, machine woven in white

cotton with a raised design to imitate the effects of quilting, which was produced at a time when 'machine made' implied 'modern'.

During the 20th century in Europe and North America there was a fashion for quilted covers; pillow shams, used for show during the day, were made to match the quilted bed cover. This was a revival of the matching quilted day-time pillow covers in use during the late 17th century.

Appliqué was worked on bed curtains throughout Europe from the 12th century until the late 19th century. They hung across the entrance to a box bed or, in a wealthier home, completely surrounded the bed, hanging from the tester. Drawn back during the day, they could be pulled around the bed for warmth and privacy at night. While sets of bed curtains were professionally made for sale to wealthy customers, many were also made by the women of the household and represented many hours of skilled work. Public officials and royalty frequently conducted business in the bed chamber, access to which was considered a privilege, so the bed furnishing, both curtains and cover, needed to reflect the wealth and status of the owner. When European colonists settled in North America they took with them the fashion for decorated bed furnishings.

In 20th-century Australia the indigenous quilts were 'waggas'; utilitarian and

ABOVE, LEFT; AND ABOVE, RIGHT: Welsh wool-suiting frame quilt, 19th century; 20th-century pieced cotton Amish quilt from Indiana, North America. This design is known as Bear Paw.

LEFT: English eight-point medallion Star within a Star, typical of the design attributed to Elizabeth Sanderson, a North Country quilt marker of the late 19th and early 20th centuries.

OPPOSITE; AND DETAIL: American Log Cabin quilt made from silks, satins, velvets and ribbons, early 20th century. The 'logs' have been sewn onto a background fabric to create a design known as Light and Dark or Sunshine and Shadow.

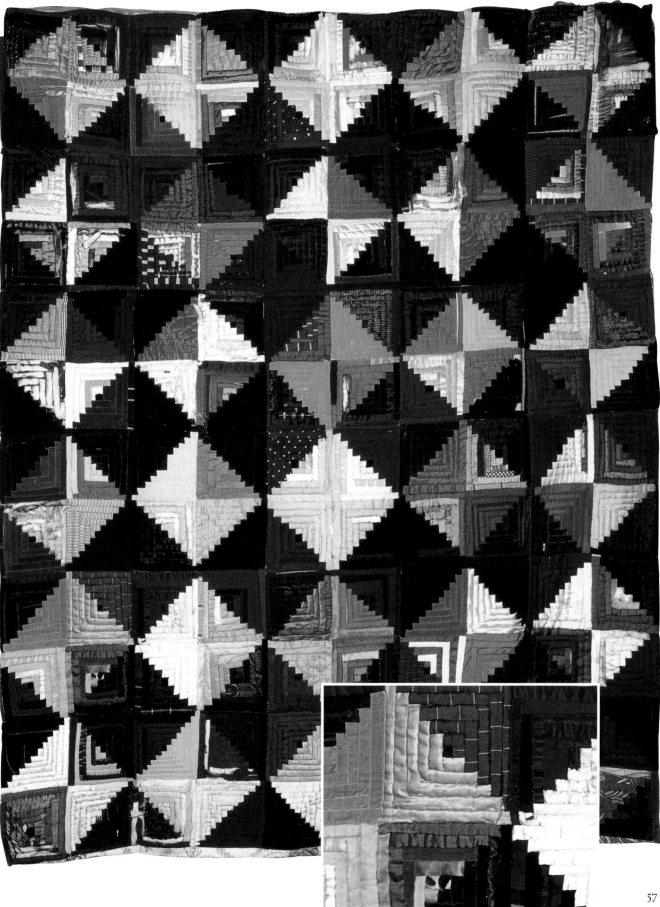

LEFT: *North Country cotton sateen wholecloth quilt, England, early 20th century.*

ABOVE, RIGHT: *Detail showing a hand-quilted design of stylized floral forms.*

BELOW: *Tanzanian quilt made up of multiples of the same block design, a variation of the North American design known as Jacob's Ladder. Each block has been separated with a pieced sashing, creating a secondary design.*

LEFT: *North Country cotton sateen wholecloth quilt, England, early 20th century.*

ABOVE, RIGHT: *Detail showing a hand-quilted design of stylized floral forms.*

BELOW: *Tanzanian quilt made up of multiples of the same block design, a variation of the North American design known as Jacob's Ladder. Each block has been separated with a pieced sashing, creating a secondary design.*

often extremely crude, they were mainly used in the country as bed quilts and verandah quilts by drovers and swagmen. Waggas were made from food sacks, cut-down clothing or woollen samples, but sometimes cotton fabrics were sewn together in a patchwork design and quilted. They were constructed all over Australia by both men and women.

Throughout Asia, a quilted cloth had the advantage of being easily rolled up or folded during the day – useful in limited living space – and easily transported, a necessity for nomadic peoples. Old, worn bedding quilts were also employed to wrap precious, fragile items for transportation or to cover animals through the cold night. In north-western India, the rural communities still fold and stack bedding quilts during the day, covering the pile of folded quilts with a decorated cover called

ABOVE: *Appliquéd and embroidered* dharaniyo *from north-west India; stylized birds and flowers are typical of both embroidery and appliqué from Saurashtra, Gujarat. The Tree of Life is worked as one of the motifs.*

a *dharaniyo*. This *dharaniyo* was obligatory in a traditional dowry and though the practice of an extensive, hand-embroidered dowry is now declining, a *dharaniyo* is still a requirement of a well-appointed village home and an object of pride to the maker, since her skills are displayed to all who enter the house during the day. It is very often decorated with appliqué as well as embroidery.

The futon, the traditional heavy wadded sleeping mat made in Japan, required

ABOVE: *Distinctive* yogi ralli *made by the Sami caste in Sind, Pakistan; with rows of concentric stitching, these are sometimes known as snake charmer quilts.*

59

TWO

HOUSEHOLD

Opposite, above, left; and opposite, below, right: *Recycled Japanese boro textile, with sashiko stitching in fan designs, used as a cover for a futon; leather cushion from a ceremonial stool once belonging to King Gizo of Dahomey, West Africa. The cushion is made from tanned and non-tanned deerskin.*

Above: *Bold appliqué and reverse appliqué decorate this* dharaniyo, *from Gujarat, north-west India, used to cover folded bedding during the day.*

Left: Katab *quilts displayed for sale in India – both tourists and locals will buy well-made textiles.*

Right: *Patchwork* takia *(bolster cover) from Rajasthan, north-west India, of silk and cotton fabrics.*

a cover. They were usually made from indigo-dyed coarse cotton, which replaced the coarse hemp and plant fibres previously used. They were often constructed from pieces of old cloth, stitched together and rudimentarily decorated with running stitch, which became, in turn, the ordered, exacting geometric pattern of traditional *sashiko* quilting.

Seating

Cushions and bolsters, sometimes simply functional, are more often an object of decoration or a display of wealth, made to show the needlework skills of the women of the household. Throughout the Indian subcontinent and the Middle East cushions were once a required part of a bride's dowry, displayed to visitors at the wedding ceremony. In Greece and the Balkan states, these cushions would usually be embroidered, but in Asia the bolsters and cushions were frequently appliquéd as well as embroidered. This enabled small scraps of expensive silk or velvet fabric, perhaps left over from other items of the dowry, to be used up.

In sub-Saharan Africa, the chief's stool, a symbol of status, could be further enhanced by a cushion, decorated in a manner befitting its owner's rank.

Cushion making in Europe and, since the arrival of Europeans, in North America, has largely followed current fashions in needlework – surface embroidery giving way to Berlin woolwork and then in the 19th century to all forms of needlework including quilting, appliqué and patchwork. A cushion is a small enough project to be finished reasonably quickly and its small size means the materials will not be too expensive; because of these two factors the cushion may be changed as soon as the fashion changes, without being too wasteful. Designs abounded – as indeed they still do – in women's domestic magazines. For instance, crazy patchwork was in vogue for cushions as for many other objects, in the last quarter of the 19th century, while Italian corded quilting and trapunto were favourites in the first half of the 20th century. Single patchwork blocks may be made into cushions.

TEXTILES, SOFT, warm and tactile, are ideal as functional or decorative coverings for walls, floors, door and window openings. Because fabric can be folded or rolled, textile furnishings are as practical for nomadic peoples as for settled communities. Practically, textiles can insulate dwellings from heat or cold or screen the interior from the sun or prying eyes. Or textiles may be purely decorative, chosen to display wealth, fashion or good taste, or the accomplishment and skill of the women of the household; or to emphasize a particular feature – the main doorway, for example. In 18th-century Europe quilted fabric was used as a lining for coach interiors. Examples can still be seen of cord-quilted designs on quilted curtains made at this time.

BELOW: *Floor covering of layers of printed cotton, the pattern of the fabric almost obscured by the stitching worked in acrylic knitting wool through all the layers, northern India.*

OPPOSITE, ABOVE: *Uzbek inlaid appliqué felt carpet, probably from Turkey.*

OPPOSITE, BELOW: *Modern wall hanging of bold appliqué and mirrors from Rajasthan, India.*

TWO

HOUSEHOLD

Floor coverings

FLOORING must be hardwearing and therefore was usually woven or knotted pile, or fur or hide, although throughout Central Asia, Turkey and Russia, thick felt is used to make rugs which may be appliquéd, either conventional or inlay appliqué, or may simply be layers of felt stitched together in a semblance of quilting. These easily portable floor coverings add greatly to the comfort and warmth of a *ger* or *yurt* during winter.

The layered and stitched Sami cloths, the *yogi ralli* of Pakistan, while usually used as bedding, are also used as eating cloths, that is, cloths spread on the ground when food is served and as cloths to cover the ground for seating. *Kanthas* from Bengal and Bangladesh and quilted cloths from north-west India are also employed in this way.

The religious community of the Amish in North America did not use carpets as they were forbidden by their religion, but some sub-groups of the Amish make small rugs from left-over fabric. They are similar to the hooked rag rugs made in Britain during the 19th century and yet they also have some affiliation to patchwork. The

LEFT: *GANESH-TAPAN*, A SHRINE CLOTH FROM GUJARAT, NORTH-WEST INDIA.

Amish rugs are made of pleated strips or triangles of new cloth – the pieces left over from larger projects – machine stitched to a backing to make a loose, coarse 'pile'. Since the purpose of these small rugs, used on the porch and in the doorway of every room, is to remove dirt from shoes, it is important that the pile is as absorbent as possible. To facilitate this, the cloth pieces are generally left with raw edges, as is the cloth on which they are stitched. While scraps left from making clothing are usually used, sometimes small pieces of patterned fabric, which the Amish would not wear, but may have been purchased in a mixed lot of mill ends, are permitted in the rug. Similar rugs, made of folded triangles of fabric stitched in concentric circles to a backing fabric, were also made by non Amish women; these rugs bear a superficial resemblance to mitred patchwork. In North America and Europe in the 1930s and 1940s the cloth from men's old suits, worn flannelette shirts or sheeting and stockings were used to create rugs for extra warmth in the home. If quilted onto an old sack it was known as Thrift quilting.

Curtains and wall hangings

A WALL hanging or curtain is necessarily a large item, and the making of it may be simplified by constructing it from several smaller pieces, finally assembling it into a larger finished whole. A wall hanging with appliquéd designs of felted wool was discovered in a grave in southern

Siberia, dating from around 900 BC. Wall hangings, large or small, using traditional indigenous textile skills are now a popular tourist item. In North America the Hmong peoples have discovered a new audience for their reverse appliqué art work and *pa ndau* textiles are being pieced together to create wall hangings. Traditional bright, primary colour schemes have been replaced by pastels and earth colours to appeal to modern Western taste, and the traditional designs have been simplified.

Pieces of silk, especially the *abr* (ikat) silk, so popular in Central Asia, are joined to make curtains and hangings. Its jewel-like colours are ideally suited to the use of small pieces of cloth as decoration. Wall hangings are sometimes made to decorate the inside of a tent; the large inlay appliqué cloths from Resht, northern Iran, were originally made by professional workers for this purpose, but now they are made to be sold. The large appliquéd cotton hangings created in the Street of the

Tentmakers in Cairo are also the product of professional workshops. Apprentices start on smaller hangings or cushion covers – usually sold to tourists – before moving on to larger and more complex pieces. The decoration may be Islamic geometric patterns, echoing the designs of

ABOVE, LEFT: Chakla *or square wall hanging heavily covered in appliqué designs, with a black reverse appliqué border surrounding the embroidered centre panel, north-west India.*

fine Islamic tiling, or may be Pharaonic scenes; very occasionally, a hanging is made decorated solely with calligraphy.

In northern India, large wall hangings, again professionally made, are produced solely for decorating wedding halls or marquees. These wedding hall cloths are appliquéd and then covered in sequins of many colours – the sequins are a cheap and quickly attached replacement for the more traditional *shisha* glass. They are brightly coloured and glitter from hundreds of points of reflected light – the overall effect in a marquee or hall, lit at night, is dazzling.

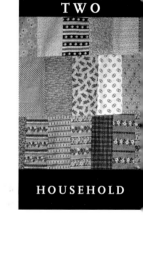

ABOVE, LEFT: *Large panel of coarse wool cloth with inlay appliqué borders and motif, typical of the work from Resht, Iran.*

TOP RIGHT: *Cotton* chakla *with a central motif of reverse appliqué and pieced borders, from Rajasthan, north-west India.*

OPPOSITE, RIGHT: Dharaniyo *in typical* katab *patterns with the four daisy motif in the top strip. Probably made from larger pieces cut down, India.*

RIGHT: Dharaniyo *from north-west India. A saw-toothed appliqué border surrounds the embroidered and appliquéd Tree of Life and figures.*

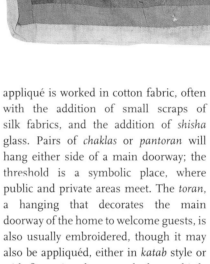

Both nomadic and settled populations of the Indian subcontinent and Central Asia make delicate window screens of small squares of silk, joined only at the corners and often further embellished with beads, with tassels at the lower edges. In a similar style, in north-west India a small wall hanging, known as a *pantoran*, has a section of appliqué or embroidery with a panel of small pieced squares hanging from it. They are often made in pairs, as are the square wall hangings known as *chaklas*. The women of the household create them for use in the home or as part of a dowry.

Door coverings

Each tribal group has its own style of decoration and while *chaklas* are very often embroidered, appliqué is also used, particularly the daisy-like *katab*. The appliqué is worked in cotton fabric, often with the addition of small scraps of silk fabrics, and the addition of *shisha* glass. Pairs of *chaklas* or *pantoran* will hang either side of a main doorway; the threshold is a symbolic place, where public and private areas meet. The *toran*, a hanging that decorates the main doorway of the home to welcome guests, is also usually embroidered, though it may also be appliquéd, either in *katab* style or with figurative shapes – elephants, birds and flowers. The *toran* is traditionally a wide strip with pennants, representing mango leaves, hanging from it. The 'leaves' symbolize hospitality and good fortune. If more than one *toran* is owned by the household, the others will hang over interior doorways. A long frieze, with pennant shapes hanging from it, called a *palli*, hangs on a wall at the point where wall meets ceiling. Appliqué is usual for such a piece since it is quicker to execute than embroidery.

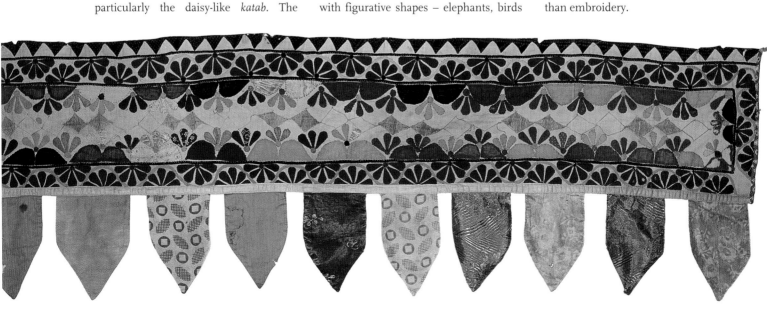

OPPOSITE, ABOVE, LEFT: *Black
and white cotton* chakla; *both the
colouring and the motif are
unusual, north-west India.*

OPPOSITE, ABOVE, RIGHT: *This* chakla
*has the most complex of the daisy-like motifs
typical of* katab. *The sixteen daisy shapes are
made from a square of cloth, folded and cut as
one piece, north-west India.*

ABOVE; AND OPPOSITE,
BELOW: *Pantoran with
appliqué, usually made in
pairs to hang either side
of a doorway, from Bhuj,
Gujarat, north-west India;
section of a* palli *used to
decorate a wall at ceiling
height, north-west India.*

Quilting, with an inner layer of
wadding, is ideal as a flexible cloth
covering to retain heat; among the
nomadic peoples of Mongolia and Central
Asia, a quilted felt panel forms a door
covering for the entrance to the *ger* or *yurt*.
With a felt door there is no need for a
middle layer of wadding – the felt itself
is thick enough to provide the necessary
insulation; the quilting stabilizes the felt,
as well as being decorative.

Quilts have always been used as a
source of warmth, but they were also used
as curtains and door coverings when living
conditions were more primitive and times
were hard. For the log cabin homes in
North America they were hung at doors
and windows to conserve heat. However,
today many contemporary quilts made
in North America, Europe and Australia
are intended to be hung on a wall, as an art
object rather than a functional item.

Bags and storage

Bags, large or small, functional or decorative, have always been needed for the carrying of goods or personal items. Nomadic peoples, in particular, require large, strong bags in which household objects may be packed and small bags for the day to day storage of goods in an environment where conventional storage such as chests and cupboards are impractical.

Bags, purses and wrapping cloths are frequently made from cloth, felt and leather. Large, hardwearing examples can be used to stow goods on a pack animal, or small, highly decorative examples may be worn for show or given as gifts. The larger and more utilitarian the bag, the more likely it is to be made of felt of several layers; felted bags are often decorated with appliqué, the layered fabric heavily quilted both to hold the layers together and to strengthen the finished object.

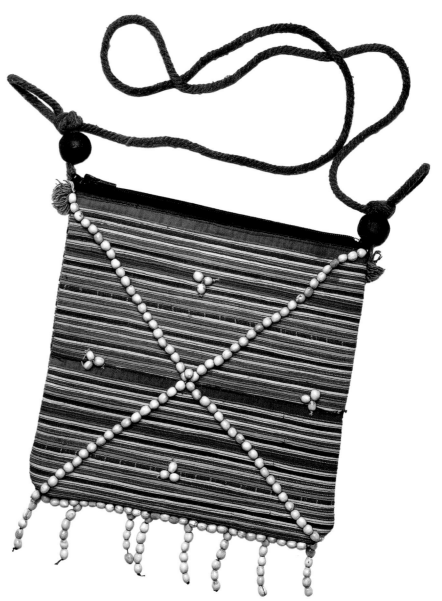

The nomadic pastoralists of Central Asia and Mongolia make and use large woven or felt bags; the latter often decorated with curling ram's horn designs in appliquéd felt or embroidery. A 'horse' bag is only found in this region, but it is actually a felt bag used to cover the ends of the framework of the *yurt* or *ger* when it is dismantled and being transported. In a region where trees are scarce, wooden bowls and other wooden utensils are precious, stored in purpose-made bags. Other bags are used to store salt and porcelain bowls.

Small, highly decorative bags are made for carrying money, tobacco or personal effects. A woman will have a tiny, beaded and embroidered bag to contain kohl, and other bags with her comb, mirror and earrings. Small exquisitely worked bags are often given as gifts, for instance, when a guest or family member embarks on a journey. These little bags, with embroidery, fringing and beadwork, are

OPPOSITE, TOP LEFT; OPPOSITE, BELOW; ABOVE, LEFT; AND ABOVE, RIGHT: *Akha shoulder bag from northern Thailand; Lisu bag made from folded and machine-stitched patchwork with Job's tears seeds, northern Thailand; typical* katab *appliqué decorates this dowry bag, Pakistan; minute Lisu bag, northern Thailand.*

almost amuletic, conveying a wish for protection on the journey.

Throughout the Indian subcontinent decorated bags form part of the traditional dowry, including a bag or purse made for the bridegroom by the bride to be. The Rabari bride makes a bag for the groom, in which he keeps sweets or tobacco, to be distributed to guests at the wedding

ceremony. In the past, every rural bride would have a number of bags as part of her dowry, worked by her and other female relatives. Today, the elaborate and time-consuming dowry is becoming a custom of the past; the dowry contains many fewer items and some will have been bought rather than made within the household.

The Banjara people of central and southern India make bags of many different shapes; once nomadic, many Banjara are now living in permanent settlements, but still retain the many layered, quilted storage bags, and the smaller pocketed bags for spices or personal effects, that were once a necessary part of their nomadic lifestyle.

Part of the wedding celebration in eastern Russia used to be the breaking of a new loaf of bread by the married couple;

BELOW: *A* masala potla, *each of the four sides is used to store packets of spices. Decorated with embellished quilting, cloth tassels and cowrie shells, typical of bags made by the Banjara people of India.*

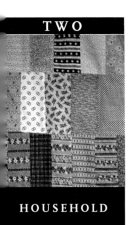

this loaf was taken to the wedding in a square envelope-style bag, known as a bread bag. Dowry bags in northern India are the same shape.

Some traditional styles of oriental dress do not allow for pockets, or one's occupation, or the objects needed to be carried, may make pockets impractical, so a bag is needed. Among the hill tribes of northern Thailand, even the everyday bag is decorated; the Akha in particular make bags decorated in the same manner as the men's and women's jackets, embellished with rows of appliqué and strands of beads or Job's tear seeds. The young men of the Lisu people make elaborately decorated 'courting

bags', worn when the man is ready to marry and looking for a suitable wife.

Another, simpler, and perhaps older, variation of the carrying or storage bag is the wrapping cloth: made to wrap and store precious objects, to carry loads, or to cover gifts offered at a wedding or at a shrine or temple. The Banjara make wrapping cloths, *rumals*, to cover

gifts of food or money. Small, square *kanthas* are used as wrapping or covering cloths.

In Japan carrying cloths were made with *sashiko* quilting on the corners, to strengthen the fabric where it would be tied in a knot.

Pojagi are the Korean wrapping cloths; made in several different styles in silk,

ABOVE, LEFT; AND ABOVE, RIGHT: *Small Banjara wrapping or covering cloth quilted with contrasting thread. The quilting is then embellished by threading a contrasting thread through the surface stitching; hardwearing storage bag with layers of cotton fabric quilted in strong cotton thread, used for transporting precious items, also made by the Banjara of central and southern India.*

FAR LEFT: *Wool-felt bag with inlaid design embellished with stitching, Hungary.*

NEAR LEFT: *Pouch of wool felt, with inlay appliqué in ram's horn design, typical of Central Asia.*

cotton, ramie hemp or even waxed paper, they were made for many purposes. Each type of *pojagi* had its own name and traditional use. Many were made for wedding ceremonies, in particular, to wrap the pair of wooden ducks presented to the bride. There is a saying in Korean: 'good fortune can be captured inside a *pojagi*'.

ABOVE, LEFT: Furoshiki, *a wrapping or carrying cloth from Japan, of indigo-dyed cotton cloth with* sashiko *quilting reinforcing the corners.*

ABOVE, RIGHT: *Patterns for quilted handbags from a small booklet of craft projects, 1930s.*

LEFT: *Quilted felt pouch, from Hungary, with a leather loop for a belt.*

RIGHT: *Bag made from a pojagi or wrapping cloth. The* pojagi *was perhaps too worn to be used as a cloth and so been remade into a bag, Korea.*

71

EPHEMERA

PATCHWORK, QUILTING and appliqué have all been used for the decoration of small household items or personal trivia. Almost entirely a leisure activity during the 19th century in Europe and North America, now the making of such small trinkets occurs in many countries for the tourist trade or for export. While this trade may preserve an indigenous textile skill, the items produced very often bear little resemblance to the original use of the technique.

The West

DURING the 19th century in the West there was a growth in domestic hobbies among women of the middle and upper classes to fill their leisure time. Crazy patchwork was a very popular craft used for all manner of small domestic items. The number of women's magazines increased and they contained instructions and patterns for the home needlewoman.

During the 1930s and 1940s there was a quilting revival in the West and patterns appeared in books and magazines, encouraging the making of slippers, nightdress cases, handkerchief sachets, tea cosies, pot holders and table linen. Just before World War II materials were in short supply and luxury items, including toys, became scarce and this brought about the return of the home-made soft toy. Scraps of material were turned into utilitarian cuddly toys.

During the Depression in the 1930s women were encouraged to create accessories, including berets, cravats, gauntlet gloves and handbags, to brighten up their clothing. New artificial silks and velvets were available, with sturdy wool and cotton poplin for items likely to have

TWO

HOUSEHOLD

BELOW, LEFT: *Small box produced for the tourist trade and marketed through a Fair Trade organization. The design is quilted with a running stitch in the same way as the traditional* kanthas *of Bengal in India.*

RIGHT: *American fashion doll in traditional Lisu dress; made by the Lisu of northern Thailand to sell to tourists.*

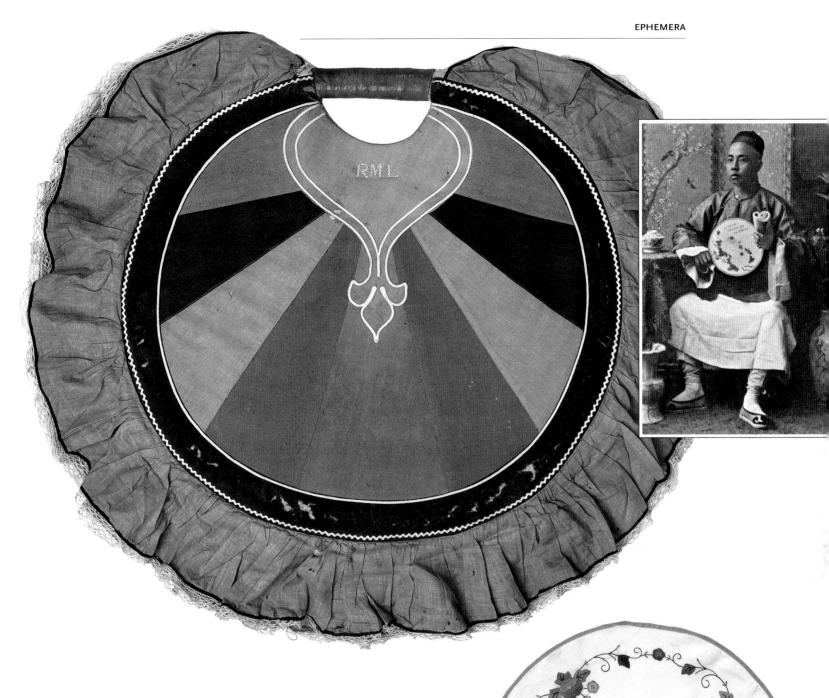

ABOVE, LEFT: *Fan, from India, of cotton fabric stretched over a ring of cane. The centre of the fan is pieced with an appliqué motif.*

ABOVE, RIGHT: *Chinese man with shoes decorated with appliqué motifs.*

RIGHT: *Dressing table mats with a floral appliqué motif; one produced in China for the export market and the other produced in England, 20th century.*

heavier use – for instance, shopping bags and handbags. Machine quilting was a means of speeding up the process and 'cord quilting' or 'Italian quilting' had been revived and was a popular means of creating a textured design. It remained in vogue for several decades.

Today, in North America the Hmong peoples from Thailand are making *pa ndau* textiles that reflect their new home. Instead of being used to decorate clothing, squares of the traditional reverse appliqué are made into pot holders, shoulder bags, tea cosies and tablecloths.

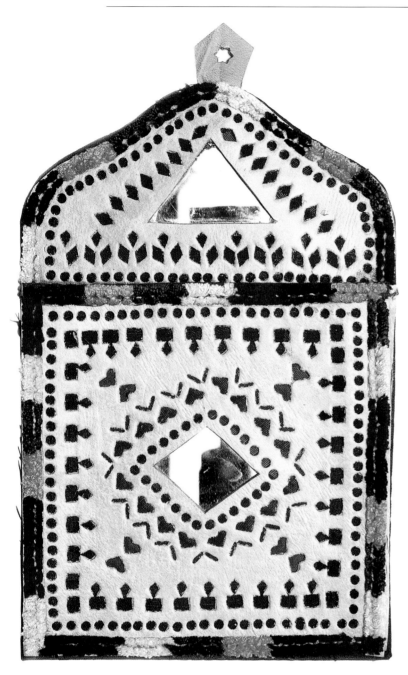

ABOVE, LEFT; AND ABOVE, RIGHT; *Mirror with cut-out camel leather appliqué, Gujarat, north-west India, 20th century; Bai child's hat with intricate appliqué and metal images for protection, south-western China.*

Following the success of an exhibition, *The Quilts of Gee's Bend* in Houston, in 2002, which promoted the quilts of African-American women from an economically depressed community, a line of home products has been developed to reflect their bold images in bed linen, table linen, ceramic tiles and a range of decorative accessories, including socks. The quilts created are also being translated into rug designs; some of the proceeds from the sale of these products will go back into the Gee's Bend Foundation, to help the community who created the original quilts.

Africa

IN southern Africa appliqué is a long established method of decorating fabrics and is still employed in the production of textiles for the retail trade. Cotton tablecloths and household linens are worked with simple, unsophisticated shapes inspired by animals and birds in the rural landscape. Today, the tentmakers of Egypt are diversifying into producing household items such as tea towels and tablecloths, decorated with their appliqué motifs.

Much of the work of preserving and reworking traditional techniques to make small saleable items is done by international aid agencies or local charitable foundations as a means of generating income for communities struggling to survive.

Four-sided Tea Cosy

Kettle Holder

TOP; FAR LEFT; LEFT; AND ABOVE, RIGHT:
Late 19th-century English crazy patchwork tea cosies of dress silks and velvets, edged with feather-stitch embroidery; cut-work felt appliquéd book cover, Eastern European, 20th century; Indian cotton book cover with patchwork, quilting and appliqué, made for export; 1930s pattern for a quilted tea cosy and kettle holder.

RECYCLED

PATCHWORK HAS its origins in recycling. Patchwork quilts were not made from new fabric, but from horded scraps, traveller's samples of cloth and shirtings and worn clothing. They were a way of extending the use of a scarce resource. Fabric would never be thrown away – it was too precious and something could always be made from it. Heavier weight fabric would also be re-used and could well become a rug, with a hessian sack as the base fabric. When a Utility quilt wore out, it too would be recycled and would most likely become the padding in a new quilt.

evidence of geometric soldiers' and sailors' quilts being made from the same uniform fabric. In the 19th century rags were shipped from Britain to other parts of the world and, in particular, to the colonies. Trade cloth included new and second-hand fabrics, and much of this was used in patchwork and quilting such as the Asafo flags of the Fante people in coastal Ghana.

The British Isles

IN the 19th century every minute scrap of precious silk and velvets became highly decorated works of art, in the form of the crazy patchwork produced by Victorian women. When Indian chintz materials were scarce, motifs were carefully cut out to become Broderie Perse appliquéd quilts. Scraps of uniform fabrics were made into decorative inlaid hangings, generally by tailors in Britain, and there is ample

609   601

805

651

922

999

600

965

OPPOSITE, TOP; OPPOSITE, BELOW, LEFT;
OPPOSITE, BELOW, RIGHT; ABOVE; AND
RIGHT: *Fragment of an English utility quilt;
English patchwork quilt of flannelette shirting;
simple cotton patchwork, from England, put
together in strips; contents of a pattern book of
numbered samples re-used to make a quilt; modern
quilt made out of plastic carrier bags and quilted
by machine, by Sally Stone from York, England.*

The Sudan

I N late 19th-century Sudan the army of
the Mahdi, an Islamic religious leader,
originally wore roughly patched garments
to symbolize poverty and humility. These
later became formalized by the army

RIGHT; AND BELOW: *Two Indian bags made by the Banjara who frequently re-use textiles. The left-hand one is made from a bed quilt, the right from a quilted wrapping cloth; botra, from Jarkand state, India, made from many layers of old sari fabrics, stitched together to make a hardwearing mat.*

officers into a white garment, decorated with symbolic applied patches of blue and brown.

India

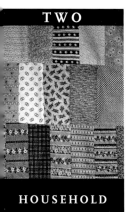

TWO

HOUSEHOLD

IN the Indian state of West Bengal and neighbouring Bangladesh, *kanthas* were originally made from old saris and dhotis, the traditional wear for men and women. Threads pulled from the woven border were used for the quilt's embroidery and quilting. In this way the textile was both decorative and functional and extremely soft. Larger *kanthas* are used as quilts and can have as many as five or six layers of old fabrics. Smaller *kanthas* are used as covers for books, cushion covers and bags, and sometimes only have two layers; because both the material and threads are old and well washed, there is no danger of dyes transferring to the lighter coloured background.

Japan

Iɴ Japan, recycling was a vital activity from the 19th century on, as individual households sought to extend the life of their possessions. Worn areas of a kimono would be patched over, with rows of *sashiko*, or running stitches used for reinforcement and to quilt layers of worn cloth together. This process of reworking textiles, with piecing, patching, mending and stitching became a domestic tradition, generally referred to as *boro* or 'ragged', where objects continue to be repaired far beyond their normal lifespan. Today, these *boro* textiles, often futon covers, are regarded as works of art and a cultural record of homespun cloth.

North America

Iɴ 19th- and early 20th-century rural North America the cotton sacks used to contain animal feed, flour or sugar, or other dry goods, were a source of printed cotton fabric used for children's clothing, aprons, household items and, of course, to piece a quilt top. The printing on plain-coloured sacks could be bleached out and the resulting white cotton used as a backing fabric for Log Cabin patchwork, or for table linen. The flour and feed mills, realizing the popularity of the fabric sacks, began to sell the goods packed in attractive printed cotton bags; these prints were in demand for children's dresses as well as for piecing into a quilt. Women would hold 'bag parties' to exchange fabric pieces.

Another use of an otherwise unlikely source of fabric for a quilt during the early 20th century, also in North America, was the sock top, as bags of unfinished sock tops could be bought cheaply from mills. The coloured bands were stitched together into long tubes, which were then sewn together, and quilted through both layers, the double layer of knitted fabric making other wadding unnecessary.

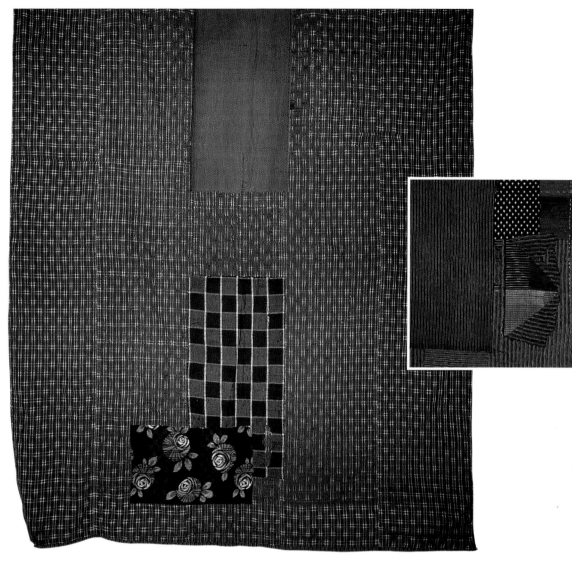

Korea

Oʟᴅ quilts are given a new lease of life on the catwalk today, where battered and worn textiles are re-quilted, sometimes appliquéd, but their origins are still obvious. Korean techniques for reconstructing cloths are being used as a means of paying homage to the past. Pieces of old quilts are being re-sewn into useable items and sold as bags, cushions and garments in high street stores. Old linen, with edgings of hand-made lace, is being dyed and incorporated into a range of household quilted items; nothing is being wasted.

Around the world, in many cultures, found objects are being used in different ways. Strange materials are appearing in quilts which are not necessarily meant for beds. Tin cans, bottle tops and litter are being made into hangings; plastic is used in place of fabric and papers and turned into quilts, of sorts. But they are not functional – they are a modern art form!

Aʙᴏᴠᴇ, ʟᴇꜰᴛ; ᴛᴏᴘ ʀɪɢʜᴛ (ᴀɴᴅ ᴅᴇᴛᴀɪʟ); ᴀɴᴅ ᴀʙᴏᴠᴇ, ʀɪɢʜᴛ: *Detail of a* kantha, *from Bangladesh, using layers of soft, old, cotton fabrics and stitched with the threads pulled out of old saris; Japanese* kotatsu, *a cloth covering a table with a heater underneath. The cloth has been patched and repatched with pieces of* kasuri (ikat) *fabric; Japanese futon cover of indigo-dyed cotton.*

CLOTHING

BABY CLOTHING
MENSWEAR
WOMENSWEAR
WORKWEAR AND
UNIFORM

BABY CLOTHING

SPECIAL CLOTHING, cloths and carriers have always been made for babies. Babies and very young children are vulnerable and therefore needed protection from evil spirits or the evil eye. As boys were favoured, they were especially in need of protection; a boy could be dressed as a girl or dressed in ragged clothing to convince the spirits that he was of little worth. Caps for children and babies were considered necessary to their good health and have been made all over the world in diverse styles using all manner of needlework.

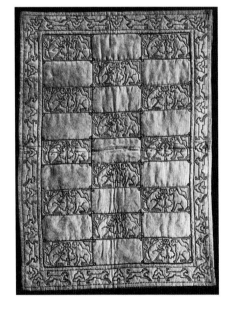

ABOVE: PATTERN
FOR A CORD QUILTED
BABY QUILT, 1930S.

Europe

IN France, the technique of trapunto was worked on various pieces of babywear, such as bonnets and bibs, and stitched pieces were used as nappies. Heart motifs were often incorporated in the stitching, symbolizing maternity. A protector quilt was provided for members of the family or friends who wished to hold the baby, to provide protection from any 'wetness'.

Many 18th-century examples of baby-wear and Christening robes have survived in Europe; some of these had been made

TOP LEFT (AND DETAIL): *Quilted baby quilt of printed fabric and Turkey Red cotton; detail of the printed fabric border, England.*

ABOVE, RIGHT: *French trapunto protector quilt with a raised central design. After stitching, the closely worked parallel lines (a feature of this kind of work) are threaded through with a quantity of cotton to create the three-dimensional effect.*

LEFT: *English satin baby quilt with a quilted design of alternate rectangles and a quilted border design.*

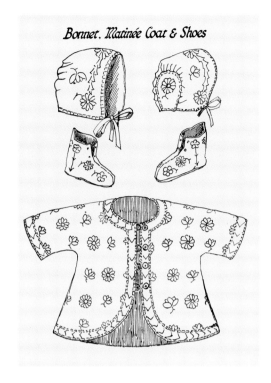

especially for the purpose, but others have been cut down from existing pieces of quilted work, usually of linen. Corded and wadded coats and jackets for infants were made throughout the 18th century along with quilted mittens. Christening garments, and especially long coats of satin, were heavily quilted.

Asia

O LD cloth, softened through wear and frequent laundering, was considered ideal for wrapping a new born child; the cloth, worn and used by the family, also conveyed a sense of community and

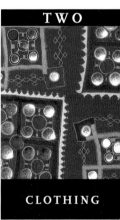

ABOVE, LEFT: *Pattern for a stitched and quilted baby's matinée set, 1930s. This was an alternative to the knitted set and was often given as a gift.*

ABOVE, RIGHT: *Child's tunic, from Afghanistan, of striped and plain cotton and ikat silk fabric with small pieced cap sleeves.*

BELOW, RIGHT (AND DETAIL): *Dress, from Palestine, made for a child from striped fabric with a decorated chest panel and appliquéd sleeves. The detail shows the patchwork and appliqué work on the neck of the dress.*

continuity. This practice is common to both the Ainu people of northern Japan and also to Bengal and Bangladesh.

In China, young children, especially boys, would traditionally be given a hat, collar and shoes shaped and decorated like animals – the tiger, a particularly auspicious animal, was one of the most popular. A collar for everyday wear or in poorer households would be less elaborate and serve as a bib as well as a decorative collar, but festival collars were often brightly coloured, decorated with appliqué, tassels, braid and beads. Likewise hats, in the form of tigers or other powerful creatures, would protect the child from evil spirits. In the past only small boys wore such hats, but today girls may wear them also. Footwear, especially the shoes worn solely for show by babies, were made in the shape of animals and

ABOVE: *Banjara cradle cloth from India. The edges are unfinished because it has never been used. The flower shapes are reminiscent of* katab *from north-western India, said to be the original home of the Banjara.*

LEFT: *Baby carrier, from south-west China, decorated with metallic braid and appliqué.*

RIGHT: *Hmong baby hat, made by the hill tribe of Thailand, decorated with a snail and a ram's head design.*

decorated with pom poms, embroidery and appliqué.

During the 19th century there was a custom of collecting small scraps of cloth from friends and family members; these pieces, each a symbol of the good wishes of the donor, would be pieced together, making a 'hundred families' coat, to protect the child from ill fortune.

Baby carriers are made by most of the indigenous peoples of south-west China; they are usually hugely decorated, with embroidery, appliqué and beadwork, each ethnic group having its own particular style of decoration.

ABOVE, LEFT; AND ABOVE, RIGHT: *Akha mother and child in festival dress, Thailand; Chinese child's hat, shaped and decorated as a fierce animal for protection.*

RIGHT: *Open-crotch trousers for a small boy, with attached boots, decorated with appliqué made to look like a fish, a symbol of plenty in China.*

BELOW, RIGHT (AND DETAIL BELOW, LEFT): *Chinese collar, traditionally worn by a boy child. Embroidered and appliquéd with silk and gilded leather to represent a protective, fierce animal.*

MENSWEAR

IN MOST cultures menswear is generally plainer and more utilitarian than womenswear. However, dress for festivals and other special occasions may be much more decorative than everyday clothing, with embroidery or braid.

Europe

IN Europe men's padded doublets, stuffed and stitched, were initially armorial garments, but later became everyday wear. An early kind of armour was the jack, a sleeved coat which had two outer fabric layers with padding and plates of metal or horn enclosed within the padding. The whole garment was laced together in a rough quilting through rows of punched holes, the lacing appearing on the outside as lines and triangles. During the 14th and

ABOVE: *A szur,* the traditional shepherd's coat of highly decorated wool-felt with appliqué, Hungary.

LEFT: *Sheepskin waistcoat with overlapping leather appliqué, Hungary.*

15th centuries the gipon, jupon, paltock or pourpoint was a high-necked, hip-length tunic, padded for protection. Usually with elbow- or full-length sleeves, they were constructed on a linen base and quilted in vertical lines to hold the lambswool padding in place. This later became a shorter, waist-length garment. In the 16th and 17th centuries, the quilting of the doublet was frequently a padded lining, the padding made of raw wool or a woollen cloth or felted wool, sandwiched between linen. The doublet fabric was silk, satin, velvet or leather. Garments of this period worn for fencing or a similar activity were quilted over the chest as a means of protection. The 18th-century man wore corded and intricately patterned, wadded waistcoats and jackets. In the 19th century coat and jacket linings were of quilted satin, as were the turned back collars and cuffs and the facings on lapels. Quilted and patchworked dressing gowns were also worn.

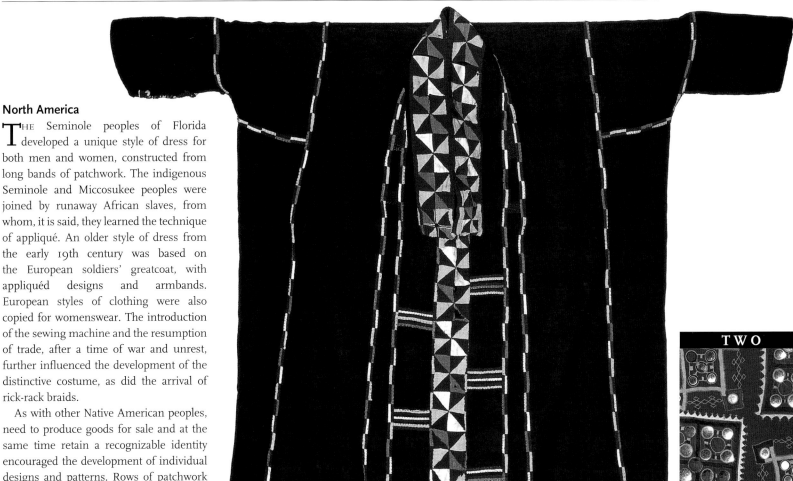

North America

THE Seminole peoples of Florida developed a unique style of dress for both men and women, constructed from long bands of patchwork. The indigenous Seminole and Miccosukee peoples were joined by runaway African slaves, from whom, it is said, they learned the technique of appliqué. An older style of dress from the early 19th century was based on the European soldiers' greatcoat, with appliquéd designs and armbands. European styles of clothing were also copied for womenswear. The introduction of the sewing machine and the resumption of trade, after a time of war and unrest, further influenced the development of the distinctive costume, as did the arrival of rick-rack braids.

As with other Native American peoples, need to produce goods for sale and at the same time retain a recognizable identity encouraged the development of individual designs and patterns. Rows of patchwork designs on men's and women's clothing in the 1920s were broad and bold. The women wore skirts with many rows of pieced strips, with a plain blouse, and a cape with a deep frill at the shoulders, the frill also containing many rows of pieced patchwork. Older styles of dress for men include leggings worn with a 'big shirt', a frock-like garment almost entirely constructed of strips of patchwork. Later clothing styles for

ABOVE: *Man's tunic, from Asia, decorated with patchwork designs. The construction lines of the garment are accentuated with patchwork strips.*

LEFT: *Bedouin man's robe, from Syria, of woollen fabric and black braid.*

men were a shirt or jacket with patchwork bands and trousers or jeans. From the 1970s fabrics other than cotton were used. Although a few people still wear patchwork for every day, it is mainly worn for ceremonial or special occasions.

Japan

IN northern Japan, kimono, leggings (*mompei*) or trousers and jackets (*sodenashi*) were necessary in a region known for protracted, cold winters. They were made of several layers, stitched

TWO

CLOTHING

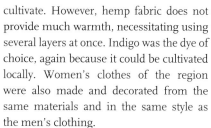

cultivate. However, hemp fabric does not provide much warmth, necessitating using several layers at once. Indigo was the dye of choice, again because it could be cultivated locally. Women's clothes of the region were also made and decorated from the same materials and in the same style as the men's clothing.

Appliquéd and embroidered coats were made by the Ainu, a distinct ethnic group living in northern Japan and on the island of Hokkaido. The traditional dress is unique, with both men and women wearing clothing of hide, fur, fishskin and cloth made of bark and other plant fibres. During the 19th century, cotton fabrics

ABOVE, LEFT; ABOVE, RIGHT; AND LEFT: *Distinctive wool-felt waistcoat from the Chitral valley, north Pakistan; Burmese man wearing a velvet coat with appliquéd design and metallic braid; Chinese man with a padded and quilted jacket.*

together; the stitching (*sashiko*) formed a decorative feature of the garment. Because of the climate cotton plants will not grow and until the end of the 19th century this region was somewhat remote and inaccessible. This has meant that most of these garments are made from hemp which could be grown locally and is easy to

own dress, language and culture; in common with many aboriginal peoples, the Ainu have had to contend with attempts to assimilate them into mainstream contemporary culture, but there is now a renewed interest in Ainu culture and a number of associations dedicated to preserving it, and there is also a renewed interest in traditional dress. The contemporary Ainu coat may contain more colours than the older clothing, but is still decorated with the same spiked and curved geometric patterns.

ABOVE, LEFT: *Plant-fibre trousers, from the Philippines, with appliquéd decoration.*

ABOVE, RIGHT: *Kuba appliqué raphia-fibre dance skirt, the Democratic Republic of the Congo.*

became available to the Ainu, who then adapted their clothing and appliqué to this new material. Bark cloth is still used, as well as cotton, to produce clothing in the traditional style of geometrically patterned appliqué in a single colour onto a plain or printed ground. The patterns of the appliqué are said to represent a spiritual and topographical map of the surrounding territory, to aid the wearer – especially if the wearer was a hunter – to find his way or to prevent him getting lost. The cotton clothing is known as *chikarkarpe*, meaning 'embroidered things'. The Ainu have their

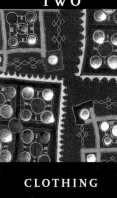

TWO

CLOTHING

LEFT: *Chinese hill tribe men's appliquéd shoes made from leather and calendered indigo-dyed cloth.*

RIGHT: *Akha man's jacket with typical embroidery and appliqué on the front, Thailand.*

WOMENSWEAR

Patchwork, quilting and appliqué have all been used on women's clothing; quilting and appliqué much more frequently than patchwork. In western Europe and post-colonial North America, the techniques have tended to be confined to particular garments or styles of garment, with the decoration changing according to fashion; a good example of this is the quilted petticoat, worn in some form or other throughout northern and western Europe for at least three centuries. By contrast, in Asia and North America the decorative techniques are specific to each tribal group, giving a distinctive and easily recognizable style of dress.

Europe

From the mid-16th century, boned and quilted corsets were an essential item of dress for almost all women in Europe. At times, the fashion was to display part of the corset, as in the Elizabethan stomacher, though for most of its history the corset was an item of underwear, to be hidden.

During the 17th and 18th centuries many types of garments were quilted. French dresses, caps and jackets have survived. The corded quilting of Provence was used for camisoles, corsets, bonnets and pockets. In other parts of Europe quilted waistcoats, bodices and jackets were fashionable.

The item of clothing most associated with the 18th century is the quilted petticoat, originally intended as a functional garment, but with the evolution of the dress style that allowed the skirts to open in the front to reveal the underneath garment, the ornately quilted petticoat became fashionable in Europe and later North America. Satin was a popular fabric for petticoats, with a fine woollen wadding and a lining of silk or a lightweight glazed woollen fabric. The quilting was usually an all-over design and very intricate, combining both cord and wadded quilting

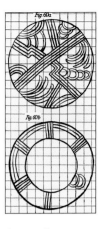

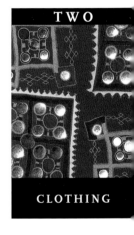

ABOVE: DIAGRAM OF A QUILTING PATTERN FOR A BERET (SEE THE DIAGRAM, BELOW, LEFT).

techniques. Garments were made from professionally quilted lengths of fabric; the fabric was also sold pre-marked with a quilting design for making up at home and they were sold by tailors and outfitters. In the Netherlands, quilted skirts, worn as both under and overskirts, were popular until the end of the 18th century along with very elaborately quilted caps. However, by the end of the 18th century quilted petticoats were no longer fashionable, but they did not disappear completely, they simply moved down the social scale. Petticoats or skirts were worn in the 19th century by fisherwomen and countrywomen. The black satin quilted petticoat was still made for the respectable woman to be buried in.

During the quilting revival of the 1930s and 1940s women were encouraged to make jackets, dressing gowns and slippers, in satin and silk.

Many garments worn today in the West are quilted and the vogue for quilted coats and jackets is comparable to the rage for the quilted petticoat in the 18th century. Quilted linings are common to many garments and outdoor wear for winter activities is of quilted waterproof and synthetic materials.

OPPOSITE, ABOVE; AND OPPOSITE, BELOW: *Woman's jumps, quilted and embroidered with the oriental-inspired floral patterns popular in England in 1740; woman's corset of blue cotton with boning and corded quilting, England, 1860s.*

ABOVE, LEFT; AND ABOVE, RIGHT: *Front and back views of English woman's stays with corded quilting to give definition and strength to the garment, 1820.*

BELOW, LEFT: *Detail of a quilted silk petticoat from England.*

BELOW, RIGHT: *English fancy dress outfit in the 18th-century style, worn at the Calico Ball, 1881.*

LEFT: THE BERET IN THE DIAGRAM (ABOVE, RIGHT) WORN WITH MATCHING CRAVAT AND GAUNTLETS.

The Americas

THE Kuna women of the San Blas Islands off Panama use an extremely unusual style of appliqué to construct their traditional blouse. It consists of two intricately worked panels of a multi-layered reverse appliqué, with a peplum and puffed sleeves of printed fabric. Early molas were more subdued in colour and were of geometric design, rather than the zoomorphic, brightly coloured molas made during the 20th century. Originally, the reverse appliqué design was just a border pattern, but gradually the appliqué was used over the entire area of the blouse panel. The mola has became a recognizable part of the Kuna Native American woman's traditional costume and shows her pride in her Kuna identity. For the past hundred years this costume has essentially remained unchanged and consists of a wrap or sarong skirt and a blouse, made up from two similar, but not identical, mola panels. It is not thought that the appliqué technique was introduced by missionaries, as it was in Polynesia – though the missionaries were probably responsible for the development of the blouse – because

TWO

CLOTHING

OPPOSITE, ABOVE; OPPOSITE, BELOW; AND ABOVE: *Section of a mola panel showing the checkerboard effect of two layers of vertical cuts, at right angles; mola panel from a woman's blouse with part of the plain fabric yoke still attached; section of a mola panel showing both saw-toothed edging and the effect obtained when a middle layer is made from pieces of many colours, all made by the Kuna people of the San Blas Islands.*

previously the Kuna women had probably not covered their upper body.

The 'Mother Hubbard', the traditional outer garment of the Canadian Inuit, was originally made of fur and hide, but by the late 19th century had an outer covering of printed cotton fabric. They could be decorated with braids and simple appliqué borders. Out of necessity, the Alaskan women added a fur edging and a large, fur-lined hood.

For the Seminole tribe of Florida, their distinctive patchwork defines their dress, for both men and women, and is therefore dealt with in the menswear section, as is the beautifully worked appliqué used on both men's and women's garments, by the Ainu of northern Japan.

Asia

The hill tribes of northern Thailand and related peoples in Burma, Laos, Vietnam and the ethnic groups of southern China all use appliqué, often very fine and intricately worked, on their traditional clothing. The larger tribal groups have a number of subgroups and those that live in different countries may be known by different names; for instance, the people known as Hmong in Thailand are known as Miao in China; this very large tribal group has numerous subdivisions in both Thailand and China, each subdivision marked by a difference in dress. The decorated clothing is almost without exception worn by the women and girls, made as festival wear. Though the younger men may have some decoration on their clothing for festivals, it is very little in comparison to the exuberantly decorated costumes of the women.

For all the numerous tribal peoples in Asia, the festival dress is of great importance; a new outfit is made each year and is as lavishly decorated as possible since it is an indicator of the family's wealth and status and, for unmarried girls, will have some influence over their suitability as a marriage partner. Today,

ABOVE; AND LEFT: *Hmong woman's jacket with delicate appliquéd stars and embroidery; Hmong girl's apron, as part of her festival dress. The central panel is batik-patterned, indigo-dyed cloth with tiny patches of cotton fabric applied, both from Thailand.*

BELOW; AND DETAIL: *Hmong girl's pleated skirt – a girl will stand or walk for hours rather than risk crushing the pleats of her skirt by sitting down. The detail of the indigo-dyed batik-patterned cloth shows tiny patches of appliquéd fabric.*

94

the costume is increasingly elaborate, though not necessarily with the same degree of painstaking skill as in the past. Increased tourism and the showy costumes of official folk dance troupes not only encourage the wearing of costume, but also encourage the use of non-traditional decoration – beadwork and sequins are now often seen – this is particularly true of the groups living in south-western China. For everyday wear, only the older or poorer people now wear traditional dress, the younger generation preferring Western or mainstream Chinese styles of clothing. This also is true of the peoples in Thailand, though tourism has had less impact on the decoration of traditional dress.

The Hmong in Thailand work a very fine form of reverse appliqué, known as *pa ndau*; the Mien, related to the Miao, use mostly embroidery, although there is some appliqué, outlined with fine braid. The Lahu, living in Thailand, use strips

LEFT: *Back view of a Lahu woman's jacket with bands of appliqué and embroidery, Thailand.*

BELOW: *Han woman's shoes for bound feet, with embroidered silk tops and delicately quilted soles, China.*

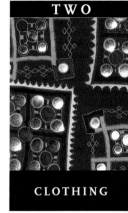

TWO

CLOTHING

of fabric appliquéd in bands, further decorated with silver beads, shells and coins. Some subgroups use very small patchwork, of squares and triangles, made into panels, and used to edge clothing. The Akha still live mostly in Yunnan, China, though large numbers live in Thailand. They have a unique dress custom as the traditional dress for girls and women changes as the girl passes from childhood, through puberty, to adulthood. In common with many other tribal peoples, the subgroups of the Akha have variations of dress, most noticeably the headdress. If the most typical item of dress for the Hmong or Miao is the pleated skirt, for the Akha woman it is her jacket. The back of the jacket is decorated with rows of saw-toothed appliqué, outlined in

LEFT: *Akha girl's hat from Thailand. This is a transitional garment; the style and shape of the hat alters as the girl passes through puberty to adulthood.*

RIGHT: *Very elaborate appliquéd and embroidered decoration on the back of an Akha woman's jacket. The tassels may be Job's tear seeds, Thailand.*

couched thread, and further decorated with embroidery and long strands of beads, coins, buttons, silver discs and cowrie shells. The same appliqué is worked onto bags and girl's caps. The Lisu use very narrow strips of folded cloth, appliquéd to the sleeve and neck openings of their garments. Many narrow strips in primary colours are used, sometimes interspersed with rows of minute folded triangles.

Another tribal group whose women's clothing makes use of appliqué is the Banjara people, now living mostly in central and southern India. As with other

ABOVE: *The traditional tight-fitting backless blouse worn by many rural tribal groups in India. This one is Banjara, the elongated triangles of appliqué being absolutely typical.*

large ethnic groups, the Banjara have many subgroups; some use embroidery rather than appliqué, some do not use appliqué at all, while others use appliqué almost exclusively. Both the embroidery and the appliqué are in the typical Banjara colour palette of dark blue, brick red, yellow, orange and maroon, with cowrie shells, large pieces of mirror, and white or metal beads frequently added as further embellishment. The appliqué is mostly elongated triangles, cut into and turned back, a skilled version of a reverse appliqué style. One interesting feature is the use of flower shapes – these are cut in

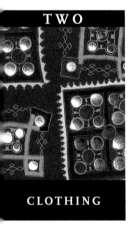

TWO

CLOTHING

RIGHT: *Banjara skirt, from India, with patchwork strips and a wide band of reverse appliqué motifs.*

the same way as the basic daisy shape of *katab*, the appliqué style from north-west India. The Banjara are considered to have originated in north-west India, travelling into central and southern India with the armies of the Emperor Aurangzeb. The women wear the full skirt (*ghaghra*) and tight fitting bodice and head shawl typical of north-west Indian rural dress. On more recently made pieces, much of the embroidery is replaced by applied strips of fabric. While Banjara women may adopt a sari for everyday wear, the traditional dress is still worn for important tribal occasions.

Quilting is used on the ubiquitous *chapan*, the quilted coat worn by men and women throughout Central Asia. From a utilitarian garment of hardwearing cotton to an elegant luxurious garment of ikat-patterned silk, the *chapan* has a long history and is still a comfortable, practical garment.

NEAR RIGHT; FAR RIGHT; BELOW, LEFT; AND BELOW, RIGHT: *Very beautiful ikat silk* chapan *– the ubiquitous outer garment of most of Central Asia; quilted sock from Korea; woman's tunic from the Swat valley, north Pakistan; Chinese musicians wearing silk garments with applied ribbons and braids.*

Workwear and uniform

WORKWEAR OR UNIFORM must be hardwearing and functional, and in the case of uniform may need to identify the wearer. Trade-related garments are also a form of uniform that advertise the occupation of the wearer.

Japan

TRADE-RELATED garments were common in Japan in the 19th century; *sashiko* quilting was traditionally used for fire-fighters' coats, fishermen's jackets and close-fitting trousers which were sometimes also patched. The fire-fighters wore a quilted coat (*sashiko hanten*), a helmet, arm and leg guards and gauntlets – all made from several layers of indigo-dyed cloth and soaked with water to give added protection from fire. The coats worn by the fishermen (*sashiko no donza*) were made up until the 1920s and were no longer worn after the 1950s with the onset of power boats; they have three layers and were often a collection of recycled, indigo-dyed pieces, roughly stitched together before being quilted or were of a finer plain or striped indigo cloth. The pattern on the shoulder was sometimes close zigzags; perhaps to echo the form of white-topped waves. On all working garments there are areas of dense stitching, increasing their hard-wearing properties. *Sashiko* stitching provided a method of reusing many materials, even rags, making them into waistcoats, jackets or backpacks. Working garments were sometimes made of larger patchwork pieces.

TWO

CLOTHING

ABOVE; AND LEFT: *Fireman's gloves, from Japan, with many layers of fabric stitched together in the sashiko technique. They would have had leather finger parts and would also have been soaked in water to protect the hands from burns; Chinese soldiers wearing quilted and appliquéd garments.*

TOP; AND OPPOSITE, BELOW: *Iscards, Kashmiri soldiers – the ceremonial headdress has been quilted, perhaps to help it hold its shape; European silk petticoat or underskirt with drawstring waist and simple quilting pattern to hem. Dark colours are serviceable for workwear.*

LEFT: *Road building in modern Afghanistan; the quilted and padded cotton trousers protect against cold and injury.*

RIGHT: *Turkomen man wearing an everyday* chapan, *the outer garment worn by all classes.*

Europe

IN 19th-century Europe, the quilted petticoat or skirt and quilted bonnet was still worn by fisherwomen and countrywomen working on the land. Working petticoats were made of stout materials suitable for outdoor wear – for instance, homespun wool; with cotton and flannel for lighter work. These quilted petticoats were extremely practical and had a patterned area of border above the hemline, created using a simple filling pattern such as the square or diamond up to the waistband.

Military garments

QUILTING has been often used for military garments, to provide warmth and padding underneath armour or chain mail or as a protective outer layer. These quilted outer garments could be made from heavy linen or leather and were designed to stop a blow, but not impede the movements of its wearer. The officers in the army of the Mahdi in 19th-century Sudan wore a uniform that had its origins in the patched clothing of the Sufi holy men, but had been formalized into a white garment with applied patchwork of blue and brown.

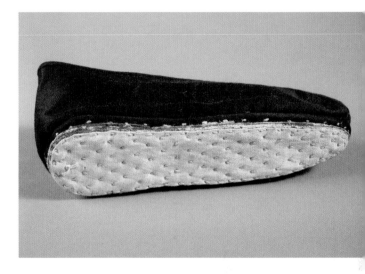

RIGHT: *Chinese cotton peasant woman's shoe with quilted cotton sole, late 19th century.*

BELOW, RIGHT: *An Indian prince wearing a magnificent uniform with decoration of applied metallic braid, 1897.*

Christ was once offered to bear the sins of many
And as it is appointed unto men once to die but hafter this the judgement · So
blood hath eternal life and I
Cleanse your hands ye sinners and purify your
For thy names sake O Lor

RITUAL AND CEREMONIAL

MARRIAGE
OTHER RITES OF
PASSAGE
FLAGS AND BANNERS
RELIGIOUS OBJECTS
POLITICAL AND
PROTEST
ANIMAL TRAPPINGS

MARRIAGE

QUILTS HAVE always been given to mark a special occasion, particularly a marriage. In North America an Album quilt, where each block was made by a different person, was often given to a bride as a gift. An early mail order pattern source, the Ladies Art Company, printed its first catalogue in 1898, and again in 1928. Certain block names show that they were planned as marriage quilts: the Steps to the Altar block and the Single Wedding ring appeared in the 1898 catalogue and Double Wedding Ring and Indian Wedding Ring in the second. The Double Wedding Ring has long been a traditional pattern made in celebration of a wedding or anniversary. The pattern first appeared in the late 19th century, but became a popular design in North America and Europe in the 1920s. Its popularity may stem from the fact that the patchwork design of interlocking rings could be made from scraps of fabric during a time of depression.

BELOW, LEFT: *Glittering Indian wedding shawl, from Hyderabad, Andhra Pradesh, of tinsel and metallic ribbon applied to net.*

BELOW, RIGHT: *Salmon-skin marriage coat from eastern Siberia; the skins of sixty salmon were used to make this garment. The skin for the appliqué has been painted in red, black and blue.*

OPPOSITE, LEFT: *Dowry bag decorated with katab appliqué; the central square is typical of a style of appliqué used for wedding canopies in India.*

OPPOSITE, RIGHT: *Banjara dowry bag with an embellished quilting design, India.*

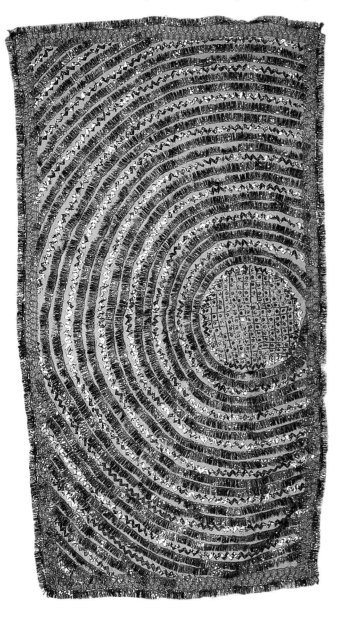

MARRIAGE quilts, or Bride's quilts, are often very elaborate and decorated with hearts, flowers and doves. The rose and, in particular, the Rose of Sharon, has come to be associated with marriage quilts. The bridal wreath is the most delicate of wreath appliqués, the circle showing the life cycle and the flowers symbolizing the regeneration of life. Hearts, appliquéd or quilted, have become a symbol of affection. If they were sewn onto a quilt before a girl became engaged, it was thought that she would never marry.

A quilt was never regarded as finished until it had been quilted. Quilts in a girl's bottom drawer, or hope chest, were not finished until she became engaged. A quilted border design on a wedding quilt must always be complete and unbroken, since broken ends could signify trouble in a marriage, which was why circles and circular wreath and flower patterns were

popular designs. In European quilts, the pattern of double diagonal quilted lines was sometimes called the matrimony pattern.

Europe

IN Europe, the bride to be would have been expected to have made a number of household textiles – sheets, curtains, bed covers, clothing – for her wedding trousseau.

In Sweden, cushions, dating from the mid-18th century, were used specifically within the wedding ceremony. They were generally pieced in triangles, squares and rectangles, sometimes with a star centre and were frequently made of a woollen fabric.

In France, the elaborate decoration of French trapunto was kept for special clothing and quilts. Young Provençal girls made marriage petticoats and quilts for their hope chest. The marriage petticoat would be worn under the dress, which was tucked up on one side to display the petticoat to its full advantage. Motifs, symbolizing love, with intertwined or highly patterned hearts, birds in the nest and flowers, were stitched alongside the attributes of a mistress of the house, such as keys and scissors, with cups overflowing with fruits and flowers to encompass blessings of abundance and fertility. On the marriage quilts, baskets of flowers, often in the four corners, were symbolic of wedded prosperity and oak leaves and fountains of youth symbolized longevity. The invention of the sewing machine brought most of this fine work to an end.

In Northern Ireland during the 19th century, the quilt itself could form part of the ritual of engagement and marriage. When the quilt top had been completed, women would gather together to finish the final stitching of the layers of top, wadding and backing. These were social affairs and the finished quilt was usually intended for an engaged girl in the community, who would be invited to the gathering. When the stitching was finished, singing and dancing would commence and the evening would often finish with the traditional 'tossing the quilt' where a girl would be 'caught', rolled in the quilt and tossed between the men. Traditionally, the girl in the quilt would be the next to marry.

Asia

THROUGHOUT most of Asia, textiles are still an important part of either the bride's dowry or of the wedding ceremony, or both. Throughout the Indian subcontinent, it is still expected that a rural bride will produce clothing and textiles for her future home. Though often embroidered, many of these traditional dowry textiles use patchwork, quilting and appliqué alongside the more usual types of embroidery. These textiles are displayed during the wedding celebration, thus demonstrating the skill and industry of the bride and her family, since the female members of the extended family will help with the making of the dowry gifts. A good display brings honour to the family and will gain her respect in her husband's household.

In northern India cloths used to decorate the wedding hall are made professionally. Since they are not intended for a great deal of wear the fabrics may be an eclectic mix of cotton and synthetics, covered with sequins of different shapes and colours. Nevertheless, despite the minimal work involved and their hurried execution, the overall effect of a hall or marquee hung round with these hangings and lit by artificial light – since weddings begin in the evening – is of brilliance and opulence.

Baby carriers made by Thai hill tribes and the Chinese ethnic minorities are an important part of the dowry.

TWO

RITUAL AND CEREMONIAL

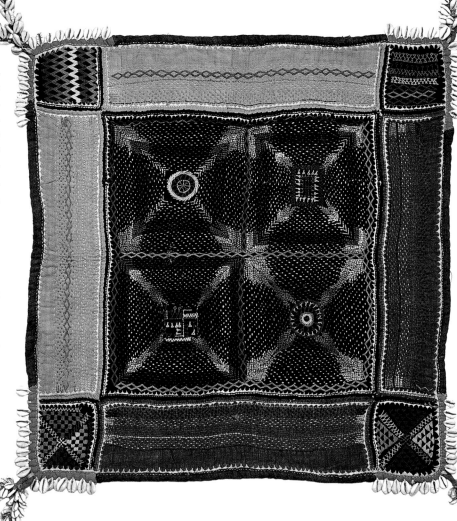

ABOVE: *Banjara cloth* dherane, *a pieced and quilted cotton wedding seat, India.*

LEFT: *Wedding pillow of velvet with additional embroidery in metallic threads, Palestine.*

OPPOSITE, ABOVE, LEFT: *Glittery cloth, from northern India, used to decorate a wedding hall; a reverse appliquéd design covered in sequins.*

OPPOSITE, ABOVE, RIGHT: *Professionally made reverse appliqué hanging; these are made to decorate wedding halls in northern India. Under electric light the sequins sparkle, creating a feeling of opulence.*

OPPOSITE, BELOW: *Inlay appliqué cotton marriage blanket, from south-west China, made by the Zhuaig tribe, mid-20th century.*

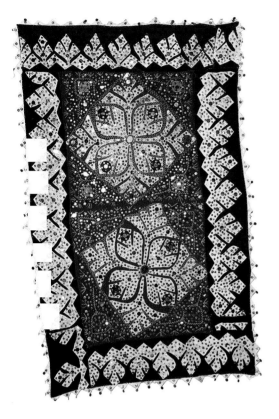

OTHER RITES OF PASSAGE

BELOW: Kantha, *from Bangladesh, portraying elephants, one of the symbols of material wealth. It therefore conveys a wish for the recipient to be prosperous.*

OPPOSITE, ABOVE, LEFT: Kantha *with floral borders and a lotus-like central motif, India.*

I N ALL parts of the world textiles, in one form or another, have played a significant role in rites of passage. They have been used to cover and embellish, from altars, beds and all parts of the home to animals, especially during festivals, and for significant life events – birth, childhood, education, coming of age, marriage and death. Women around the world have made quilts to mark significant events in their families' lives, the ties of friendship, events in their community and religious occasions.

TWO

RITUAL AND CEREMONIAL

Childbirth

A s early as the 13th century in France, 'warmers' were listed in royal inventories. This was a type of linen, quilted in the trapunto manner which was used during childbirth. It was warmed and placed on the stomach of the woman in labour.

Quilting, patchwork and appliquéd cloths have been made for babies, as can be seen with European cot quilts and christening layettes. In Bengal, a *kantha* would be stitched for a new-born child or for a daughter to take when she married and moved to her in-laws' home. Here, symbols of plenty and fertility are combined with combs and mirrors and

symbols of married women; horses and elephants are symbols of material wealth. Later, when the child had become a mother or grandmother herself, she would portray the same objects for another girl-child.

Special occasions

I N Turkey quilts have been professionally made by men for special occasions such as the circumcision of a boy-child; the women of the family would personalize the quilt by adding good luck tokens or talismans such as coins or turquoise ornaments to ward off the evil eye.

Patchwork quilts have also taken on meanings that are unique to members of the Native American communities. A quilt is

frequently given in ceremonies called 'Giveaways'. In the Plains region, Giveaways are often held by families for baby-naming ceremonies, weddings, graduations and memorial feasts for the dead. These memorial feasts take place approximately one year after the death and could involve as many as three hundred guests and the giving of up to one hundred quilts.

The *ta taura* style of *tivaivai* are given at a ceremony marking the making of a new household and, although they are large enough to fit on a double bed, they tend not to be used as a decorative coverlet, but are kept for ceremonial occasions and given as gifts to those leaving home or to express respect, love or loss.

The pieced style of *tivaivai* is intended as a personal possession, made by the quilter and it would either wrap the quilter's body in death, or it would be given to a favoured family member.

Death

D EATH is marked by a specific range of textiles, for instance, in Nigeria funerary shrine cloths of patchwork and appliqué have been made since the 19th century. In the Native American culture of the Great Lakes, shirts and skirts accompany the dead; they are decorated with cut ribbonwork which symbolizes the whole person being split – half in this world and half in the spirit world. In the West, in the 19th century, a mourning wardrobe of clothes was always needed. Silk mourning pictures were made and sometimes a Memorial or Mourning quilt; these are frequently embroidered with dates of birth and death and mostly date from the second half of the 19th century. Made in sombre

colours of black, white and grey, very often with a black border, the quilt was used during the period of mourning, or as a Memorial quilt, to commemorate the life of a family member or friend who had recently died. These mourning quilts could be passed around among family members as the need arose. The Memorial quilt, by contrast, was not necessarily quite so sombre, as portions of the clothes of the deceased person were frequently incorporated into the quilt. A widow might use portions of her wedding dress as well as pieces of her husband's clothing. Objects of significance to the deceased person were sometimes worked into the design.

A century later, in North America, the 'names' project began in 1987, to commemorate those who had died of AIDS. The 'AIDS quilt' is assembled from a series of panels, each representing the size of an adult body. The number of panels is now so great that it is impossible to display them all in one place. In less than a decade the number of panels had grown to more than thirty thousand, including panels from many other countries as well as North America. While some panels make overtly political statements, many are in the style of the 19th-century mourning quilt, containing pieces of clothing and objects of significance to the deceased or the mourners. Just as in the 19th century, relatives have found comfort through the construction of a commemorative cloth.

ABOVE, RIGHT; AND DETAIL: *Tent hanging, for ceremonial occasions, made in the Street of the Tentmakers in Cairo, Egypt. The detail shows an Islamic tile pattern.*

BELOW, RIGHT: *Tent hanging, Cairo, Egypt.*

FLAGS AND BANNERS

E VERY COUNTRY has its own national flag and where the design of the flag uses large areas of solid colour, this is almost always achieved by piecing together the sections of different colours.

West Africa

I N West Africa there is a tradition of producing banners and flags decorated with appliqué. In the 15th century coastal Ghana (formerly the Gold Coast) was a centre for trade in gold and ivory and later, slaves. Within the Ashanti empire the Fante tribes already had their own military companies, known as Asafo (war people), for defence. European colonization brought with it European military companies. The Fante took on the heraldic and military flags and adapted them to suit their own needs and culture. They formed into companies which were given different names and numbers, with proverbs (African history is traditionally told in proverbs) and an image to convey power, victory and ferocity; these were used to taunt rival companies. Until their independence, in 1957, they also displayed the European flag of the appropriate occupying power; today, they display the Ghanaian flag.

The flags are all double sided and made of trade cloth, mostly with appliquéd images inlaid. Although the majority are cotton, some include felt, wool and silk. The themes fall into four categories: historical events and victories, plants and animals used as metaphors, symbols of European military and industrial domination and illustrations of proverbs. During festivals and funerals the flags become banners and shrine decorations.

Further east along the West African coast, the Fon of Benin were a people of ancient Dahomey. Between the 16th and 18th centuries they were the main exporter of slaves to Europe and the West Indies. The men spun the cotton and made colourful hangings and flags or

ABOVE: *Chinese bride seated in front of a large banner with appliquéd characters.*

BELOW: *English commemorative banner made by the pupils of Flamborough School, Bridlington, Yorkshire, in March 1887.*

banners. The Fon flags are narrative, using images of people, animals or mythological symbols. To these motifs were added scenes of people fighting with sidearms and muskets. In 1850 there were bloody civil wars and tradition demanded human sacrifices. The memory of these massacres is still depicted in the banners. The appliqué makers were part of a cloth-working guild mainly employed by the chiefs, who would commission a banner with symbols that represented something about themselves. The motifs were kept by the guild so that the next generation could have the old banner remade with the addition of new symbols. The banners normally stay with the chief, but they are brought out and hung up at festivals and ceremonies. On the whole, the background is dark with brightly coloured cotton pieces, cut out using templates and hemstitched in place. Embroidery stitches are added for decoration.

Europe

THE military colours still used by European regiments are mostly embroidered, but the battle honours are double-sided appliqué in silk fabric. These are painstakingly applied by hand.

Tibet

TIBETAN Buddhist monasteries are hung with textiles, including Victory Banners, which are tall, cylindrical hangings composed of many tasselled pennants, made of silk brocade. The five colours (green, blue, yellow, white and red) represent the five Buddhist elements.

ABOVE, LEFT: *Company number three flag, made by the Fante people of West Africa, with appliquéd allegorical detail. It also includes the Union Flag belonging to Britain, the occupying power, 19th century.*

ABOVE, RIGHT; AND BELOW: *Cotton flag of number two company, made by the Fante of West Africa, with a patchwork border and an appliquéd allegorical design; cigarette silks have been made into a quilt, Ontario, Canada, early 20th century.*

RELIGIOUS OBJECTS

THE MOTIFS, colours and even the fabric used in a patchwork, quilted or appliquéd item can have symbolic meanings. In North America, the plain, deep colours and matt surfaces found in old Amish quilts symbolized their humility and dedication to God. Many of the older Amish quilts are of a woollen cloth, which gave the finished quilt a matt surface. Some quilts have a deliberate mistake in them since it was believed that a perfect quilt might offend God. The Amish quilt should not be considered a religious object, but it is a functional item whose decoration reflects the spiritual orientation of the Amish society. Within the Amish, Mennonite and Pennsylvania German peoples who came to North America certain familiar, folk-art symbols are incorporated into their quilts. Quilt motifs illustrate different aspects of their faith. Christ is represented through the use of the rose, the heart, the star, symbolizing his birth, the diamond, representing Christ as the rock, and the tulip, which is a popularized form of the lily. The central diamond, often the focal point of an Amish quilt, reflects the idea that Christ is the focal point in a household. The 'Sunshine and Shadow' quilt pattern is said to represent the night of sin and guilt and the bright shining light of Grace.

Native American

NATIVE American peoples have adapted the beadwork, rug and basketweaving patterns of their cultural heritage into their quilts. The medicine wheel, an ancient religious symbol, is often used as a quilting pattern. When broken into four quarters, the wheel represents the four stages of life, the four directions, the elements and the four seasons.

Kanthas

RELIGION and folk belief have been extremely strong influences on the *kantha* and the choice of material used. The *kantha* is made of rags; it represents a sense of unity because it is constructed

from different parts, like the pieced robes of Buddhist monks. There are different traditions of *kantha* art, whether Hindu or Muslim, but since the *kantha* revival in the early 1980s, the religious differences are gradually being eliminated. Women from Muslim backgrounds are adding in motifs that had distinct associations with Hindu mythology and similarly, Hindu women are embroidering *kanthas* that are distinctly Islamic in tone. The Muslim influence in Bengal has also created different *kantha* articles, namely, a prayer rug and an envelope-like *kantha* to cover the holy book. The most important of all

OPPOSITE; AND DETAIL: *Shrine cloth made in the 19th century to sell to visitors to the shrine of Salar Masud in Uttar Pradesh, India; the many figurative elements illustrate aspects of the legend of Salar Masud.*

ABOVE: *Large canopy, made in Pipli in the Indian state of Orissa, for use in religious processions. The central rosette uses a technique of layered, folded appliqué.*

RIGHT: *Shrine cloth or* Ganeshtapana *made in Gujarat, north-western India. Saw-toothed appliqué edges the embroidered cloth, depicting at its centre the elephant-headed Hindu god Ganesh.*

religious influences has been that of folk belief and magic, and in an agrarian community the close association of nature and human beings is reflected in designs combined on the *kantha*.

India

SINCE the 11th century appliquéd articles have been produced by professional workers for the temples in Orissa, eastern India. Much of this appliqué work was originally made in Pipli for the enormous Jagannath temple complex at Puri. Pilgrims to the temple could buy appliquéd cloths to present at the temple as offerings, or smaller cloths or canopies to take home for their own household shrine or local temple. Large canopies and umbrellas were made for religious processions. Pipli is still a centre for appliqué work, although now objects, from tablecloths, cushions and bags to small hangings are mostly produced for the tourist trade.

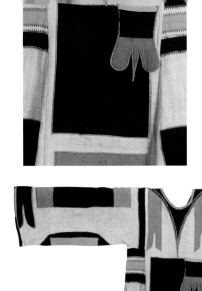

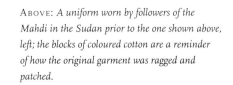

ABOVE LEFT; AND DETAIL: *Uniform of the followers of the Mahdi in Sudan, decorated with appliquéd designs, 19th century. The detail shows the distinctive pocket shape.*

LEFT: *Tibetan patchwork ritual cloth of Chinese silk brocade and damask, 18th century. The construction is similar to North American block patchwork.*

ABOVE: *A uniform worn by followers of the Mahdi in the Sudan prior to the one shown above, left; the blocks of coloured cotton are a reminder of how the original garment was ragged and patched.*

RIGHT: *Tibetan silk appliqué panel depicting a dakini in dancing pose; she is holding seven precious jewels, 17th century.*

OPPOSITE, LEFT: *Cloth of wool flannel for an altar, southern India. The details of the figures of the gods have been drawn in pen and ink.*

OPPOSITE, ABOVE, RIGHT: *Tibetan lamas; the lama on the left, a 'dancing lama', has an appliquéd upper garment.*

OPPOSITE, BELOW, RIGHT: *Temple dancers from Sri Lanka.*

Garments

DEDICATION to God can be expressed by the humility of wearing patched garments as worn by Buddhist monks and the followers of the Mahdi in Sudan in the late 19th century. The followers of the Mahdi originally dressed in ragged, patched garments, the traditional dress of Sufi initiates, to signify their detachment from worldly wealth.

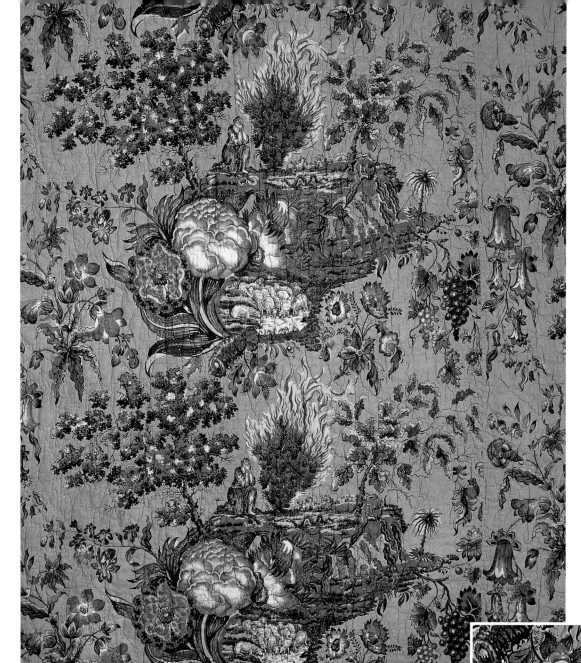

The Christian Church

From the Middle Ages the established Christian Church has been the recipient of expensive altar cloths and priestly vestments. Appliqué using velvet, silk or gold kidskin was used with gold and silver threads and semi-precious stones. During the Reformation in Europe in the 16th century there was a reaction against this outward display of wealth in the Church, but by the 19th century there was a revival of what was considered to be Medieval art which was reflected in the church furnishings of the period.

Above; and right: *Details of a quilt made in England from a very unusual printed textile. The biblical story of Moses and the burning bush is depicted among the more usual floral elements.*

Opposite: *Wool flannel table cover, with pieced and appliquéd elements and biblical verses embroidered in cross stitch. Possibly made as a group project by a church or religious community, Britain, late 19th century.*

POLITICAL AND PROTEST

BELOW, LEFT; OPPOSITE, ABOVE; AND
OPPOSITE, BELOW: *Patchwork quilt in 'patriotic'
colours, giving a flag-like quality to the central
panel, mid-20th century;* khatwa *– a silk appliqué
panel made to raise funds for a community
and as part of a campaign to promote AIDS
awareness; Fante appliquéd flag, with a warlike
theme, for a military company, West Africa.*

IN THE 19th and early 20th centuries women were denied a political voice, but through their textiles they were able to express thoughts that addressed Western social, moral and ethical issues and in doing so, laid the groundwork for the quilts of conscience from the 1960s onwards.

In the West

AMERICAN quilts, dating from the early 19th century, include themes of the early development of communities and social, political and economic issues made at a time when many women could not read or write. This was the beginning of women moving from a pattern of a home-centred existence to a community-based activity. Many historical quilts represent institutions such as the church and document social concerns, relief efforts and women's suffrage. To many activists in the suffrage movement quilts were interpreted as symbols of women's subjugation, so it seems ironic that a quilt should chronicle the activities of a suffragette. Quilts were also made as a means of fund-raising and to provide financial support in times of hardship, as can be seen with the Wholecloth quilts from the mining areas in Britain. Quilts were made to raise funds for the temperance movement; one such quilt, in red and white, appropriately takes the Drunkard's Path as its pattern. After the overthrow of the Hawaiian monarchy in 1894, to demonstrate their loyalty to the royal family, images, reminiscent of designs used on the tapa cloth, were incorporated into quilts.

Arpilleras

IN Chile, in 1973, General Augusto Pinochet seized power and between then and 1977 some 700 political prisoners disappeared. The families of the 'disappeared' used every means at their disposal to ensure that they were not forgotten. Textile crafts can play an important role in helping women to cope in an intolerable situation and *arpillera* making was a direct response to the 1973 coup and represents the way in which political

TWO

RITUAL AND
CEREMONIAL

views about lack of food, money and injustice were recorded. They became known as 'Appliqués of Protest'. They are small panels made of fabric scraps on a background of sacking or 'arpillera'. The techniques used are simple, but they are filled with scenes of life and peopled by small figures with stuffed heads and three-dimensional clothing. In the early days they contained scraps of paper with the name of the 'disappeared', or an explanation of the scene depicted. For instance, the scene depicted might be a child health and feeding programme – not uncommon in a developing country – but here necessary because of the disappearance of the family's menfolk. Many *arpilleras* show a giant sun which is not only a reality in a South American climate, but also a symbol of continuing faith. It is thought that the *arpillera* originated in Chile, from

BELOW; RIGHT; AND OPPOSITE: *Appliquéd scene of peasant labourers in Colombia; 19th-century English patchwork, appliqué and embroidered bed cover commemorating the wedding of Princess Charlotte to Prince Leopold of Saxe-Coburg and Gotha; late 19th-century Hawaiian flag quilt.*

TWO

RITUAL AND
CEREMONIAL

a tradition of wall hangings made by the political activist Violet Parra in the 1950s. She, like the *arpillera* makers two decades later, used feed sacks, small objects, wool yarn and simple appliqué in her work. The earliest *arpillera* workshops were set up by the Catholic Church as a means of helping women made destitute by the political troubles. In a traditionally male-dominated society, making the *arpilleras* gave the women a voice and an outlet for grief.

In 1980, following the Chilean example, *arpilleras* were made in Peru and Colombia, to generate an income for the makers who were displaced for political reasons and living in shanty settlements. In Peru they are sometimes called *arpilleras*, but are usually known as *cuadros* which means pictures.

South Africa

IN 1980, two members of the Zamani Soweto Sisters, an organization that oversaw township women's self-help

groups, saw an exhibition of Chilean pieces in London and it inspired them to create their own scenes of township life, as a political protest in South Africa.

AIDS quilts

'AIDS quilts are not so much bed covers, as banners, both personal and political. In 1987 they were seen as a 'unifying quilt in memory of those who had died of AIDS'. All the names of the dead would be recorded in quilt blocks. Men involved in AIDS quilts are addressing current and future issues, sticking and stapling instead of stitching, and these were shown laid on the ground. Unlike quilts to be treasured, the making of an AIDS quilt became a way to counter the stigma of homosexuality associated with AIDS.

India

IN Bihar state, northern India, *khatwa* appliqué and *sujani* – an embroidery and quilting hybrid very similar to *kantha* – is

used not only to generate income for village women, but many of the textiles now also address the social issues that the women struggle with such as AIDS, contraception, child marriage and female illiteracy.

From the 19th century textile banners were a means of showing radical dissent. They were produced by numerous organizations and were often a carefully considered political strategy. Typical among these were the campaigns for women's rights and for disarmament. With the global nature of the banner, today they can be seen to promote working for a Nuclear Free Zone and women's peace camps. Quilts today are not only functional, but are also seen as a way of expressing concern about contemporary issues. Environmental matters are addressed in both a decorative form and by incorporating items normally thrown away. Quilts have moved into the mainstream of art, carrying messages of local and global concerns.

ANIMAL TRAPPINGS

ANIMAL TRAPPINGS, broadly speaking, serve to protect an animal or to adorn an animal for a festive or religious occasion or to enhance the owner's status. Working animals may need protection from cold, or from the chafing of packs or saddles; animals used in war need protection from injury. Animals in a religious ceremony – pulling a vehicle that contains a religious image, for example – need to be appropriately adorned. Animals conveying bride or groom to or from their wedding ceremony are also caparisoned, and even working animals conveying their owner to market may be decorated to enhance or display his status. Trappings made for a functional purpose are also sometimes highly decorative; a harness may have tassels, beads and other embellishments added. These often serve a protective as well as decorative function; even today, in many societies, the movement and sound of brightly coloured adornments is considered to deflect the evil eye.

Quilting, with its combination of lightness, padding and warmth is ideal for the protection of animals and may be combined with patchwork. Appliqué produces a multi-coloured, decorated fabric that is both reasonably quick to produce and hardwearing – useful attributes for a cloth that must adorn a large animal and be used regularly.

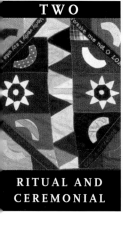

TWO

RITUAL AND CEREMONIAL

Ancient times

ANIMALS have been domesticated and herded for thousands of years; evidence of animals, especially bulls, being objects of worship dates from the time of the ancient city states of Ur and Sumer, in what is now Iraq. There is

ABOVE, RIGHT; AND BELOW: *Bullock cart, showing the animals adorned with appliquéd or embroidered* jhul: *these were usually made in matching pairs; part of a* maffa, *the tent-like covering for a square bullock cart. A new bride would be conveyed to her husband's home inside a* maffa, *protected from prying eyes.*

evidence of horse riding dating from 3000 BC. Tomb paintings from Ancient Egypt and carvings from Assyria show animals harnessed to chariots for war, harnessed to carts for transport and adorned with both functional and decorative trappings.

Asia

THE nomadic peoples of Central Asia continue to make animal trappings of felt, leather and cloth; their nomadic lifestyle requires large sturdy bags in which to pack household goods, bags to cover the ends of *yurt* poles and also coverings, harnesses and saddles for the animals themselves. In the Indian sub-continent, animals are still widely used in agriculture and for transport, and for religious ceremonies. Elephants, camels, horses and oxen may all be adorned with cloth and tassels for festive purposes.

Europe

THE peoples of Ancient Europe also used horses, oxen and asses for transport, haulage and warfare, all of which would have necessitated the making of both harnesses and decorative

ABOVE; AND RIGHT: *Tibetan yak bell and collar of woollen fabric; bullock cart: the jhul has an embroidered centre and appliquéd borders.*

BELOW, LEFT; AND BELOW, RIGHT: *Bullocks with forehead decorations and long decorated strips wound around their horns; patchwork, quilted horse armour from the Sudan, 19th century.*

ABOVE: HORSE AND BULLOCK FULLY CAPARISONED IN TRADITIONAL TRAPPINGS.

trappings. The Saami of Scandinavia and Russia still herd reindeer and make attractive felt trappings for their animals.

The Crusaders

As Islam developed the use of the horse in warfare, this made a form of protective covering both for horse and rider a necessity. A lightly padded and quilted garment was worn beneath suits of armour and a similarly padded covering helped protect the horse. Both armour and protective padding were adopted by returning Crusaders, with the result that the making of armour became one of the major industries of Medieval Europe. Alongside the craftsmen working in metal were those making the banners, surcoats and animal trappings, each bearing the heraldic device of the knight. Armour and the associated heraldic trappings became obsolete with the change in warfare due to the advent of firearms.

The Americas

Eto the Americas, and the tribes of the Great Plains in North America, in particular, quickly adopted the horse, adapting their lifestyle to it totally. As with every other horse-owning culture, the Native Americans made trappings to decorate their animals, reflecting the status of the animal's owner. In some areas of North America where dogs are still used for transport dog harnesses are also decorated. The llama, the pack animal of the Andes, is often decorated with wool tassels and carries panniers and woven bags.

RIGHT: *Horse head cover with appliquéd designs and pieced border.*

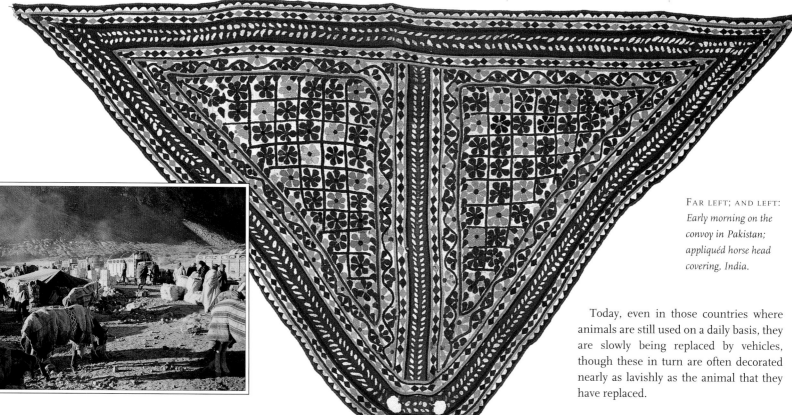

FAR LEFT; AND LEFT: *Early morning on the convoy in Pakistan; appliquéd horse head covering, India.*

Today, even in those countries where animals are still used on a daily basis, they are slowly being replaced by vehicles, though these in turn are often decorated nearly as lavishly as the animal that they have replaced.

LEFT; AND ABOVE:
Camel trapping with appliquéd designs from Rajasthan, north-western India; camel with a quilted cotton cover and a ralli (quilt) covering the saddle, India.

BELOW, LEFT; AND BELOW, RIGHT:
Patchwork camel trapping, from Central Asia, of cotton and silk ikat fabric; camel cover from Bhuj, Gujarat, north-western India. This cover, made by the Rabari people, decorates the camel that carries the bridegroom to his wedding.

TWO

RITUAL AND
CEREMONIAL

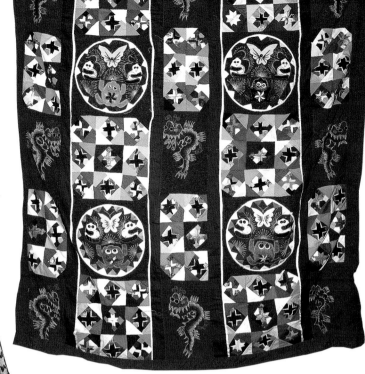

LEFT; RIGHT; BELOW, CENTRE; BELOW, LEFT; BELOW, RIGHT; AND BOTTOM: *Detail of a reverse appliqué panel, northern Thailand; patchwork and appliqué hanging from China; Chinese child's 'tiger' shoes; North American quilt in traditional Amish design; Miao jacket from East Guizhou province, China; unused shoe soles of thick layered cotton showing sashiko quilting patterns, Japan.*

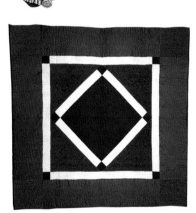

CONSTRUCTION

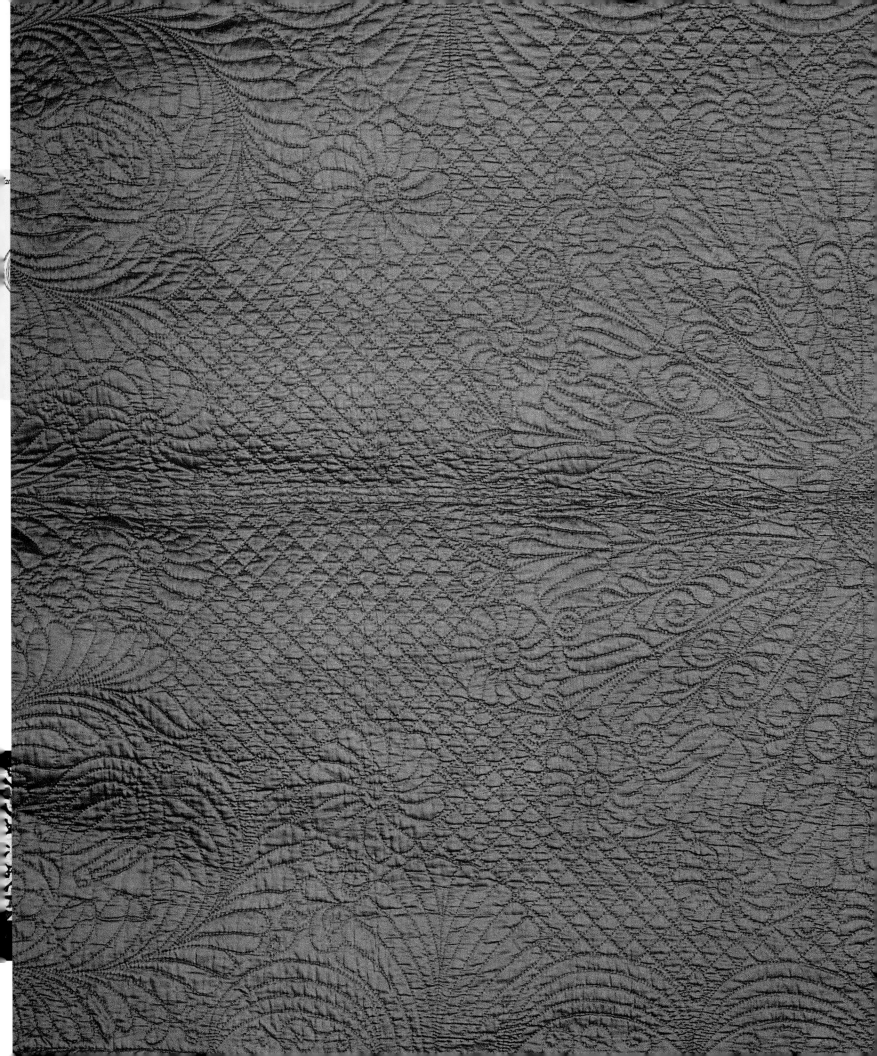

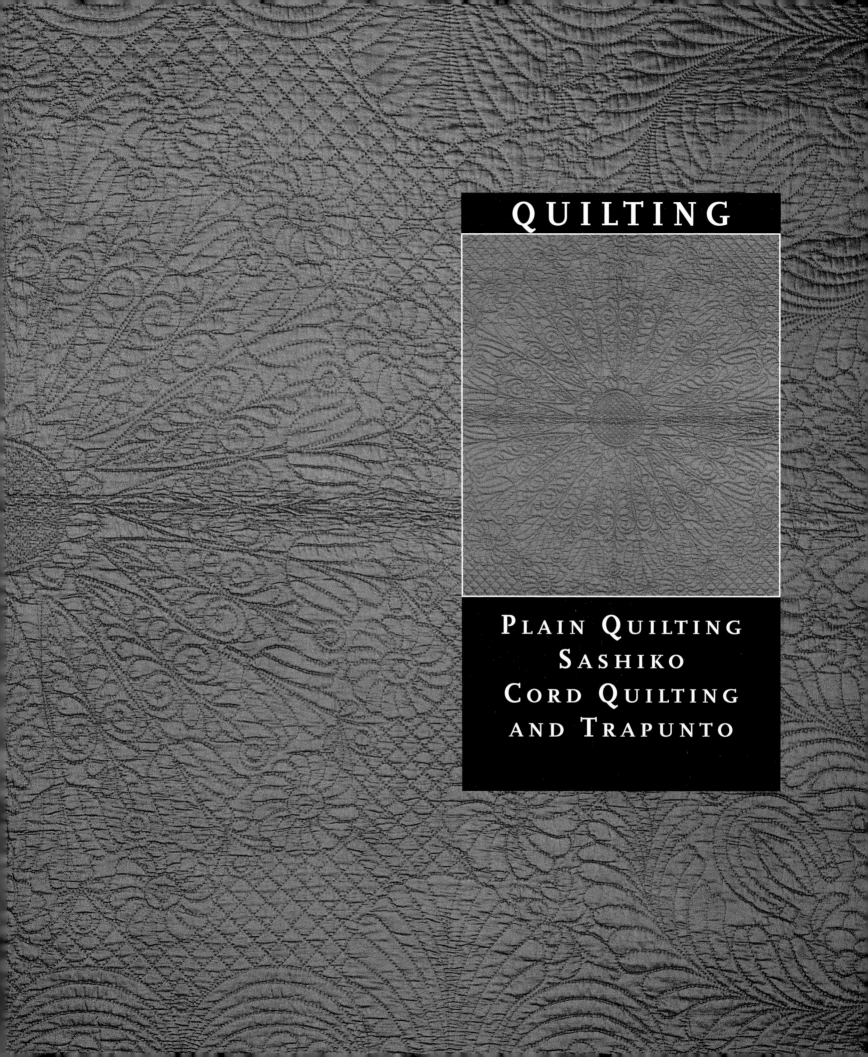

QUILTING

PLAIN QUILTING
SASHIKO
CORD QUILTING
AND TRAPUNTO

PLAIN QUILTING

INDIAN SUBCONTINENT

QUILTED and embroidered bed covers were produced during the 17th, 18th and 19th centuries at several sites in the Indian subcontinent, for export to Europe. They were of a style similar to those produced in Europe, with two layers of fine cotton fabric with a thin inner layer of wadding. The design was quilted in backstitch in a similar colour to the fabric. Bed covers from Bengal were decorated with more figurative embroidery in silk, drawing on the local tradition of *kantha* embroidery, but produced to designs that were obviously European in origin. Most bed covers were embroidered rather than quilted. In northern India the quilted designs were subtle and very obviously Mughal in origin, popular with both the home and export markets.

Ralli

THE name *ralli* means quilt and is derived from the word to mix or to join; these pieced and appliquéd quilts from Sindh in Pakistan were originally made of reused fabric. The quilting is a very simple running stitch in random colours, in straight lines across the whole body of the quilt, which holds the layers together. *Rallis* are often made as dowry gifts; the quilt top will be made by one woman or the womenfolk of one household, and then women from several other households in the community will come together to complete the quilt in a day, by first laying out and then stitching the layers together. They are made from several layers of fabric; while the fabrics

RIGHT; AND ABOVE (DETAIL): Ralli *or quilt, from Pakistan, typical in both colouring and design. The quilting is stitched, using any colour that comes to hand, in straight lines across the pieced top.*

THREE

QUILTING

130

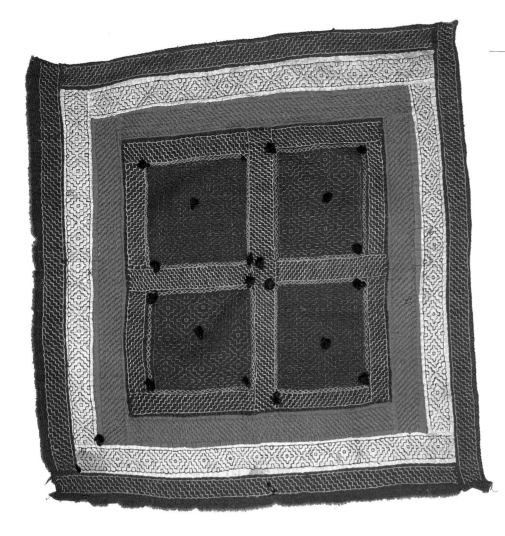

constructed from several large pieces of spare cloth, pieced together, and then stitched through all the layers. The stitching is part running-stitch quilting and part small, simple embroidery stitching, giving the finished cloth a pleasing, graphic quality and a durable, hardwearing finish. The cloths are less decorative than utilitarian, made for function rather than ornament.

Kanbiri

Quilted cloths and bags are produced in *kanbiri* stitch – this is a distinctive style in which the cloth is made up of several different-coloured strips pieced together, then the quilting is worked in black or dark thread in geometric, step-like patterns. This is worked by rows of running stitch, which are then linked with rows at right angles to the first, producing the typical patterns of *kanbiri*. In the past,

Above; and right: Wrapping cloth of kanbiri *quilting, Pakistan; bag decorated with* kanbiri *quilting, Pakistan. In the past* kanbiri *was used for precious or religious objects.*

used for the decorative top layer may be new, or mostly new cloth, the middle layer(s) and backing are quite likely to be used cloth, recycled from a previous textile.

Sami

Other forms of quilting from Pakistan are the randomly pieced and stitched cloths of the Sami caste used as bedding, wrapping cloths and mats, sometimes called a yogi *ralli*, and said to be used by snake charmers. These cloths are

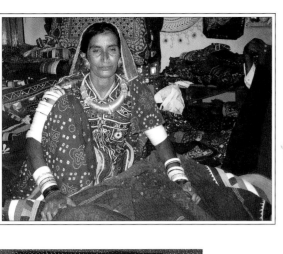

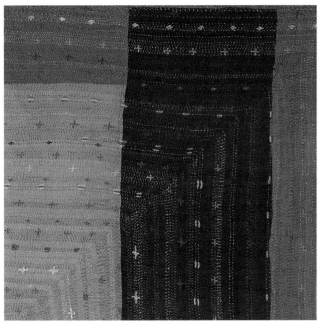

items decorated with *kanbiri* were given as gifts to religious leaders, but today this style of decoration is also used for dowry objects.

Banjara

THE Banjara people are said to be from Rajasthan in north-western India originally, but in the 17th century, as carriers to the Emperor Aurangzeb's army, they spread throughout India. As a nomadic people, they had a need for large and small bags for storage and the transport of household items as well as wrapping cloths. Square cloths for ceremonial purposes are also an important part of Banjara culture. These cloths and bags are heavily stitched with running stitch through several layers of cotton fabric. This stitching – usually done in off-white thread – is then further

RIGHT: *Detail of a modern* kantha *panel, made in colours thought to appeal to the Western market, India.*

embellished by threading a contrast-coloured thread through the stitching on the surface of the cloth in bold, simple geometric designs. This is not only pleasingly decorative, but also very durable and hardwearing. This threaded quilting is sometimes confused with *kantha* but, as the illustrations show, it is quite different. In southern India, some sub-groups of Banjara make quilts of recycled sari cloth, drawing on a local southern Indian tradition of quiltmaking. The quilts of large strips of cloth, pieced and then stitched with small embroidery patterns, are very similar in appearance to the quilts made by the Sami community of Pakistan.

Kantha

K ANTHA stitching takes the principle of quilting with embroidery still further. The name *kantha* is thought to refer to the quilt or layered cloth from Bengal or Bangladesh. In the northern Indian state of Bihar this running stitch embroidery is known as *sujani*; like *kantha*, it is worked on a layer of cotton fabric and is a form of flat quilting. In Bangladesh the term *nakshi kantha* usually indicates a *kantha* with patterns or pictorial motifs.

The cloth or quilt is first constructed with several layers, the number of layers varying according to its intended use; a cloth for summer use or a wrapping cloth will perhaps have only two or three layers of fabric, while a cloth intended as a winter bed quilt may have as many as seven layers. These are then stitched together; those intended for a gift or for show may be elaborately embroidered, while those for everyday use will be less decorative. In the most ornamental *kanthas* the body of the cloth is covered with scenes from everyday life, religious motifs, the *kalka*, the *buta*, the paisley motif, or floral patterns, all worked in coloured running stitches through all the layers of fabric. A central lotus motif is traditional and is still frequently used. The background between the coloured designs will be quilted with running stitch in a colour to match the fabric; on older quilts this is quilted around the shape of the motifs, a technique known as echo quilting, which gives a subtle textured effect to the finished piece.

In the past, *kanthas* were very much a craft born of poverty; the layers of fabric were made from old worn sari lengths, softened by wear and washing. Coloured

OPPOSITE, TOP; OPPOSITE, LEFT; OPPOSITE, ABOVE, RIGHT; AND OPPOSITE, BELOW: *Gujarati woman displaying embroidery and appliqué for sale, India; detail of a Sami ralli from Sind, Pakistan; small Banjara bag, India; wrapping cloth quilted in typical Banjara style, India.*

BELOW: Kantha *panel, which, though modern, nevertheless depicts a scene from a traditional Indian story. Two swordsmen are shown with a tiger.* Kantha *pieces have been a means of generating income for the women of rural Bangladesh.*

from both Europe and North America, alongside the famous Sanderson Star quilt design. Cotton sateen was the favoured fabric for making quilts.

Welsh quilting

Iɴ Wales quilting was part of the rural and mining communities as it was in the north of England. While in the north of England quilt tops were traditionally sent to a marker or stamper, the Welsh had itinerant quilters, who travelled from farm to farm quilting. The Welsh quilting tradition also includes the Wholecloth medallion and the strippy, as well as the pieced medallion, but many Welsh quilts have strong lines and bold colours reminiscent of those of the Amish communities in North America. Quilting designs are frequently superimposed on the pieced design rather than following the shapes. Patterns of leaves, ferns, hearts, tulips and spirals are freely adapted. Welsh quilts are very different from each other, but the predominant style seems to be one of a round centre with borders in rectangular frames; the more geometric style has continued to flourish in Wales. Welsh quilters preferred carded wool wadding rather than the prepared cotton used in the north of England. In Wales, cotton sateen was considered to be 'grand' and a much more sturdy fabric, such as wool, was more likely to be chosen, and this produced quilts with a sculptural quality.

Amish quilting

THE Amish communities came to North America from Alsace in France, Switzerland and southern Germany between 1727 and 1850. They settled mainly in Pennsylvania, Ohio and Indiana. The finest Amish quilts are made of plain, lightweight, woollen cloth or cotton fabrics, in strong colours. They combine scarlet, burgundy, emerald, rich blues, coral, purple, navy blue, black and turquoise. Their patterns are geometric, a juxtaposition of simple, striking shapes with elaborate hand-quilting patterns of curling feathers, stars, lattices, tulips and baskets of flowers, worked in black or a dark-coloured thread. In contrast to the

OPPOSITE, TOP LEFT; AND OPPOSITE, BELOW, CENTRE: *Wholecloth quilts with central designs featuring deep border patterns and a diamond background were widely found in Europe and North America.*

OPPOSITE, ABOVE; AND OPPOSITE, BOTTOM: *Feather patterns are a popular feature of North Country quilts, England, early 20th century; wholecloth medallion-style quilts were typical of the North Country tradition in England.*

ABOVE, RIGHT; NEAR RIGHT AND FAR RIGHT: *The strippy style was typical of North Country quilts with cable designs and a Weardale Chain, England, early 20th century; many Amish quilts feature scrolling feather designs; naturalistic quilting design on a silk petticoat, England, 1780s.*

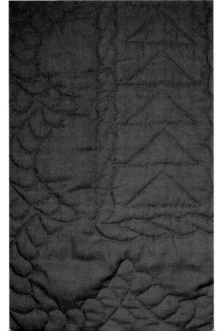

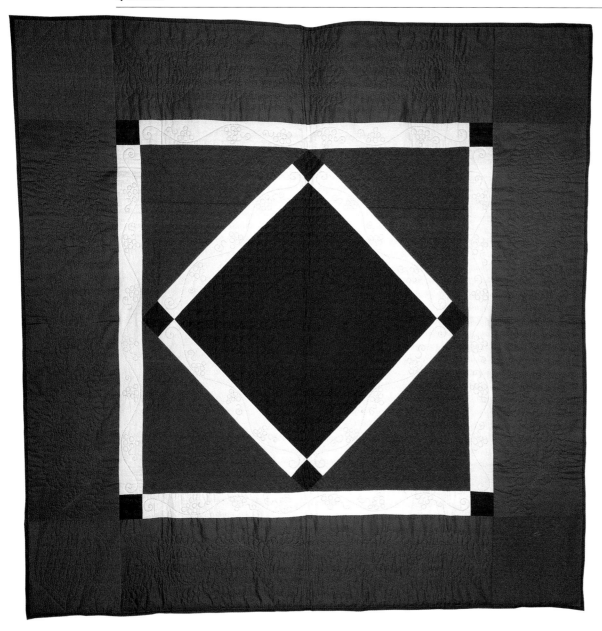

Welsh pieced quilts, the quilting directly relates to the pieced design. The quilts tend to have a wadding of thin cotton or wool, to complement the wool or cotton fabric for both the top and bottom layers. Today, there are more than 150,000 old order Amish living in twenty-two American states and in Ontario, in Canada.

Quilting today is in a very healthy state. New materials for the top fabric of the quilt and for waddings, or battings, allow a greater freedom of expression in spacing the pattern and machine quilting offers exciting possibilities and experimentation. Quilting is no longer practised out of necessity but for enjoyment.

ABOVE, LEFT: *Amish centre diamond design demonstrating the strong, distinctive colours used in this North American patchwork style. Quilting patterns were worked to fit in with the patchwork shape, stitched with a running stitch and a dark-coloured thread.*

TOP RIGHT: *Amish saw-tooth diamond design with strong contrasting colours for maximum effect, North America.*

ABOVE, RIGHT: *Detail showing quilting patterns on Amish saw-tooth patchwork, North America.*

LEFT: *Amish basket block, North America.*

FLAT QUILTING

Europe

Quilting worked on two layers of material with no wadded layer is known as flat quilting, Queen Anne or false quilting. It was one of the most common types of quilting worked in the late 17th and 18th centuries in Europe. As flat quilting is more decorative than functional, it is more at home in the manor house than the cottage. The fine work, sometimes combined with corded and stuffed quilting, and sometimes combined with embroidery, is generally done in back stitch or chain stitch, which is more time consuming than the running stitch used in wadded quilting. The materials of silk, satin, cotton and linen and the silk and linen threads were costly, and out of the reach of the cottage economy. The bottom layer, generally, is of poorer material than the top.

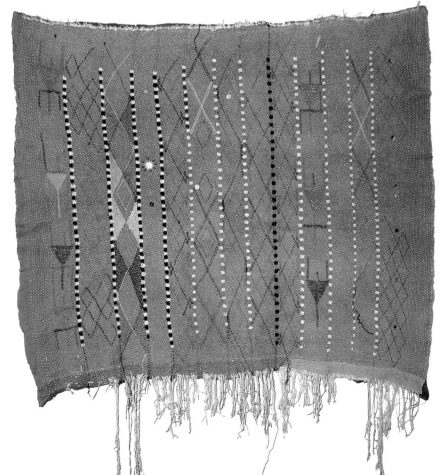

There are two distinct styles of flat quilting: the most flamboyant is the coverlets, pillows and bolsters of silk satin, backed with linen, and quilted with metal threads, with areas worked in coloured silks in long and short stitch and satin stitch. Generally these were professionally worked and incorporated floral designs, including the rose, the carnation and the tulip. The background quilting was nearly

ABOVE, LEFT; AND TOP RIGHT: *Banjara quilting showing the patterns made by threading a contrasting thread through the quilting stitches, India; detail of a quilted felt bag – although the pattern is in relief, the quilting is not wadded as only one layer of felt has been used.*

ABOVE, RIGHT; AND LEFT: *Detail of a Mongolian quilted felt mat; heavily stitched quilted cloth, from Pakistan, showing thin, stylized figures among the geometric patterning.*

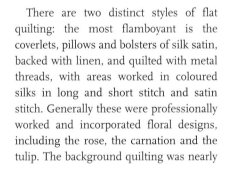

THREE

QUILTING

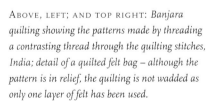

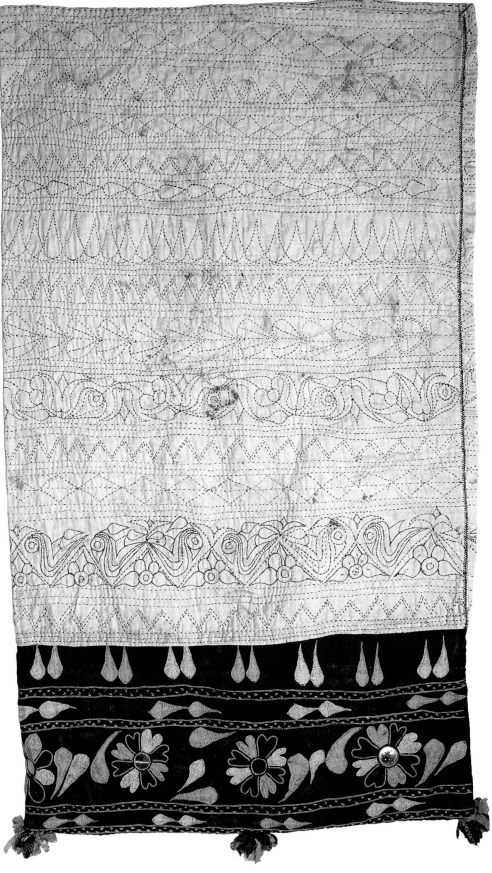

ABOVE, LEFT; AND DETAIL: *Ethnic Chinese child's hat; the body of the hat is quilted blue silk. The detail shows the appliqué design on the hat.*

RIGHT: *Flat quilted, panel dowry bag from India; the designs of running stitch quilting echo those of the embroidered border.*

OPPOSITE, ABOVE; AND OPPOSITE, BELOW (AND DETAIL): *Man's tunic, from the Swat valley, northern Pakistan. The thick cotton fabric and the dense stitching combine to make a rather stiff, unyielding garment; flat quilted cloth, from north-west India, which is a functional rather than a decorative piece of very simple construction. The motifs include two figures churning butter, a symbol of plenty. The detail shows the Tree of Life pattern and simple quilting.*

always done first. The second style of flat quilting was frequently worked with yellow silk thread, perhaps in imitation of the metal thread, on a linen ground and used for coverlets, cushions and all manner of costume accessories, especially caps for women and children. The patterns worked are similar to the designs on wadded quilting of the period and the background filling patterns seem to be universal.

SASHIKO

THE WORD *sashiko* is derived from *sashi*, meaning to stitch (a general form, practised throughout Japan) and *koginu*, the hemp fabric. It is thought that *sashiko* has been in existence since ancient times, in the form of advanced darning and patching, to extend the life of a garment. Areas of a garment that received the most wear were patched most frequently and stitched with thread made from the same fibre and since the thread did not contrast, designs were chosen primarily for utility.

The Japanese in rural areas either dyed their cloth or thread with indigo or left it undyed. Hemp gave way to cotton, in most parts of Japan, but even in those areas where hemp continued to be used, cotton thread became available and it contrasted strongly with the indigo-dyed textile used for clothing. In the 18th and 19th centuries, *sashiko* stitching began to lose its original utilitarian purpose and was practised for its decorative value. It moved up the social scale, from the peasant society to the merchant classes, and its association with mending declined.

Technique

THE technique of *sashiko* is simply one of running stitches sewn into indigo-dyed fabric with white thread, to create a variety of geometric patterns. The stitches are much more visible than in traditional Western quilting because of the contrast between thread and fabric. The designs are motifs borrowed from nature and the environment, and stylized objects. The patterns are repetitive and based on a grid of vertical, horizontal and, sometimes, diagonal lines.

Designs

A LARGE number of *sashiko* patterns came from Chinese designs, however, many of these 'Chinese' patterns had travelled via the Silk Route and the designs had actually originated in India, Persia or even Greece. Buddhism was introduced into Japan from Korea between AD 552 and 710 and some *sashiko* designs were derived from Buddhist symbols. Indigenous Japanese plants became popular as design motifs. The Hemp Leaf, or *asanoha*, pattern is a classical example; with its complex array of stitched lines, it is the strongest of all designs – appropriate because of the way the hemp plant is revered. The Hemp Leaf pattern is frequently sewn into infant clothing and bedding.

Traditionally used for work wear and functional textiles, in its characteristic indigo blue hemp or cotton, *sashiko* is classified as Mingei – the art of the people. This form of 'folk art' was first collected in Japan in the 1920s as there was a nostalgia for the past and the disappearing rural crafts. Today, it may be seen in Japanese fashions and textiles.

LEFT: *Late 19th-century Japanese fireman's coat with* sashiko *stitching. The coat would have been soaked with water for protection, while the stitched dragon would provide divine protection. During use, the plain inside of the jacket would be turned outside and the decorative dragon would be revealed after the fire was extinguished.*

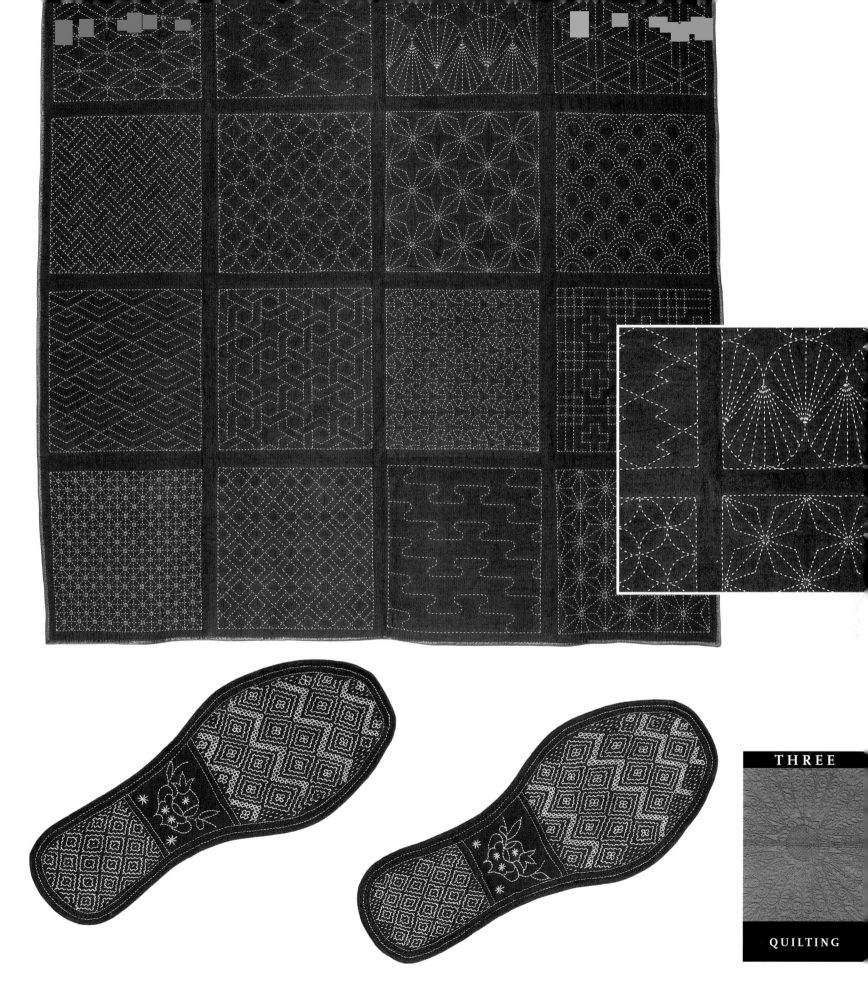

THREE

QUILTING

CORD QUILTING AND TRAPUNTO

ORD QUILTING, known in England as Italian quilting, was worked on two layers of material, usually linen, probably from the 13th century on; the design was stitched with parallel lines of backstitch or running stitch. A cotton or wool cord was then run through the channel created by the quilting stitches, from the back. Stuffed or padded quilting, also known as trapunto, was also worked on two layers of material with outline patterns stitched with backstitch or running stitch; the design elements were then stuffed by inserting a filling through a hole in the back, to provide an area of high relief. Sometimes these stuffed designs were further padded with an extra wadded layer, which was known as bas-relief quilting. Both techniques can be combined. Their intricate patterns demonstrate a high degree of skill with the needle.

BELOW, LEFT; BELOW, RIGHT (AND DETAIL); AND OPPOSITE, BELOW, LEFT: *Cord quilted bed cover, 1720–1760, stitched with a running stitch in white thread on cotton, with a range of both stylized and realistic flowers, England; English cord quilted bed cover, 1690–1720, stitched with a back stitch in yellow thread on a linen ground, with surface embroidery; cord quilted panel of black silk, late 19th century, England.*

THREE

QUILTING

ORDED quilting and stuffed quilting, was known in India, Persia and Turkey and it also developed in other parts of Europe. While wadded quilting has been looked upon as part of a 'cottage economy', corded and stuffed quilting belong to a very different background. Bed covers of wadded quilting were intended for warmth, but those with corded patterns were less practical but highly decorative. In the 13th and 14th centuries it was a popular technique in Italy, France and Spain, where it was often used for bedspreads.

Examples of 16th-century work have been discovered in India, often including

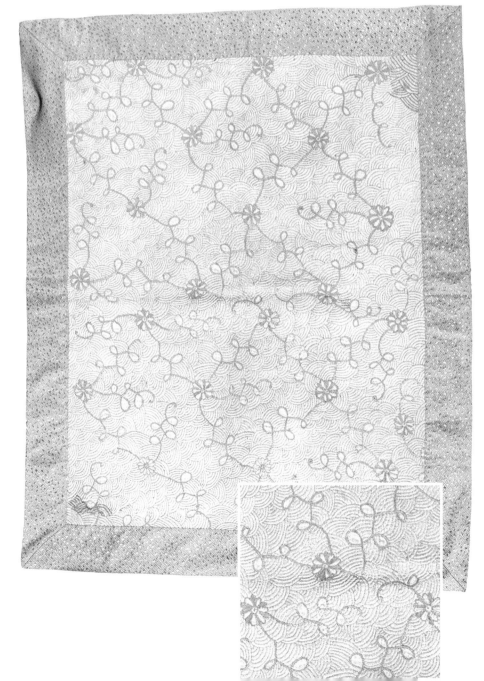

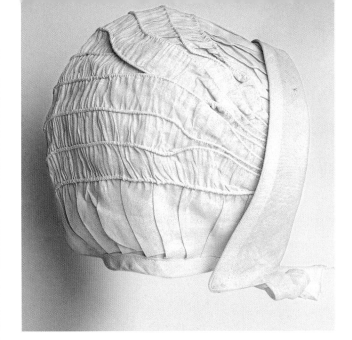

hunting scenes with figures in European dress and combining quilting with trapunto and cord quilting. The designs could have been copied from pattern books of the period and were destined for a European market. The technique of corded quilting, often combined with trapunto, reached a peak of popularity in the 17th and 18th centuries where it was used mainly to add decoration to garments, such as linen caps, women's jackets, men's waistcoats and petticoats. Patterns of naturalistic flowers and leaves were corded and combined with pulled-work techniques (a counted-thread technique) to create amazingly complex designs.

Cord quilting was also worked in Germany, Poland, the Czech Republic, the Netherlands and Scandinavia and was taken up in North America later in the 18th century. The popularity of cord quilting does not appear to have continued into the 19th century; rows of cords inserted along the bottom of a petticoat or in the brim of a bonnet bore little resemblance to the cord-quilting designs of the previous era. The technique was revived in Europe during the 1920s and 1930s with the popularity of cord-quilted cushions and other ephemera.

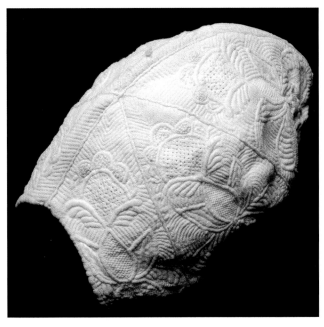

ABOVE, LEFT; TOP RIGHT; RIGHT, CENTRE; AND BELOW, RIGHT: *Quilted bonnet, similar in style to a Staithes bonnet, England, 19th century; fine organza bonnet with a simple corded design; finely quilted and trapuntoed linen cap; 18th-century cord quilted linen bonnet, all European.*

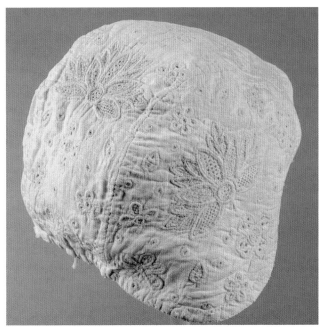

APPLIQUE

Plain Appliqué
Reverse Appliqué
Inlay Appliqué

PLAIN APPLIQUÉ

PACIFIC APPLIQUÉ

THE Pacific islands of Fiji, Papua New Guinea, Hawaii, the Cook Islands and Tahiti are halfway between Australia and California. It is thought that the population of the islands mainly came from Asia. Before the arrival of the Europeans there was no woven cloth. Instead, the islanders made tapa from the inner bark of mulberry and breadfruit saplings; after repeated poundings the fabric was the consistency of felt. Designs were painted or stamped onto the tapa and these are considered to be the forerunner of appliqués found on *tivaivai*.

The tivaivai quilt

THE *tivaivai* quilt is specific to Hawaii, Tahiti and the Cook Islands, and also to the population of these islands who have migrated elsewhere. It is uncertain when quilting began in the Pacific, but it is generally accepted that it was primarily learned through contact with Euro-American culture. Once introduced by missionary wives, the techniques, patterns and motifs spread throughout the islands of Polynesia, but quilting never supplanted the use of tapa and mats in Samoa and Tonga and was largely rejected by the islanders who lived there. Some evidence now exists that contact with African-Americans and peoples of

ABOVE; AND OPPOSITE, ABOVE, LEFT:
Woman wearing tapa cloth; stitching a cut-out tivaivai *design to its cloth backing, Cook Islands.*

Hispanic background also influenced particular patterns.

There is very little written documentation concerning 'women's work', but it is thought that the introduction of sewing and quilting came from the women who travelled to Tahiti on board *HMS Duff* in 1797. Hawaiian quilts are often considered the forerunners of Polynesian *tivaivai*, however, missionaries did not arrive in Hawaii until 1820. During the same year demand for cloth in Tahiti was so high that newly introduced cotton crops were being grown and in 1821 weaving and carding machines were in place, to make the locally grown cotton into cloth.

The earliest quilts were patchwork, taught as a simple technique, and this was closely followed by appliqué. The general population made do with whatever trade cloth they could get and used it for tiny

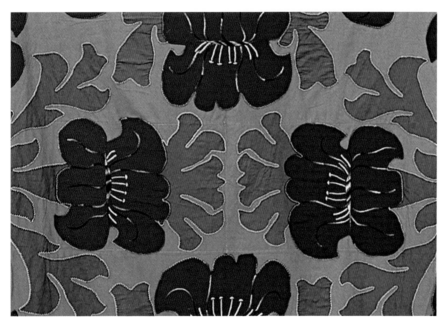

THREE

APPLIQUÉ

ABOVE, LEFT: *Floral motifs applied to a coloured background to create a symmetrical design, typical of the* ta taura *form of* tivaivai, *which originated in the Cook Islands. This modern design was made in the 1990s using cloth bought locally.*

LEFT: *The* manu *or cut-out* tivaivai *where the design is cut out in a snowflake-like manner, the patterns reflecting island flora.*

patches; early pieced *tivaivai* were often very small. The predominant colours were red and white; a bright, red cloth known as Turkey Red was the most available cloth, used as barter when trading with the islanders; but the households of the chiefs had access to cloth that was of better quality and in more plentiful supply, and this was used for appliqué.

Today, there are three types of *tivaivai*: the pieced or *taorei* is characteristic of Tahiti and the Cook Islands. Originating in the Cook Islands, the *ta taura* form of *tivaivai* show floral motifs appliquéd to a contrasting coloured background, in a symmetrical design. The motifs are copied and rotated to explore the design; these are further embroidered to give a depth to the flowers.

The third type of *tivaivai* is the *manu* or cut-out *tivaivai*. Here the fabric is folded into sections, the design drawn on and cut out in a snowflake-like manner. The production of this form of *tivaivai* is similar to the tradition of making stencilled *tapa*; the patterns reflect island flora.

Prior to the 1960s *tivaivai* were not for sale. Public sales were first limited to church projects, but with the increase in tourism the demand for *tivaivai* grew and craft associations were born.

KATAB

APPLIQUÉ IN north-west India is generally known as *katab*, though it may also be known as *khatwa* or *katao*. The word *katab* is thought to have derived from the English 'cut up', as indeed may the variations of *katao* (cut out) and *khatwa* (cut work). It is not thought to be an indigenous skill; the oldest surviving examples are only a century or so old. Appliqué is said to have been introduced through mission schools or the educational efforts of the wives of British Army officers. Whatever the origin, the style is now a distinctive, attractive appliqué, easily recognizable.

This style of appliqué is used largely on wall hangings, *dharaniyo* (covers for folded bedding) and wedding canopies. There are two separate, though related methods, which each produce a different end result. The first, and perhaps more complex and attractive, is the daisy-like repeat patterns; these are made by folding the square of – usually white – cloth into quarters, and cutting into the fabric. Depending on the intended result and the skill of the worker, this can produce a daisy of eight petals,

149

THREE

APPLIQUÉ

a group of four such daisies joined, or the most complex, a group of sixteen such daisies joined. Though at first glance this sixteen daisy motif may appear to be made from several separate units, this is not so – the whole motif is cut from a single piece of fabric. Many other variations are possible, all starting from the initial folding of the cloth.

Katab is an ideal technique: no measurement or drawing out of templates is required, yet identical repeat motifs can be made, simply by starting with squares of cloth the same size. The colours are typically, though not exclusively, white fabric on dark blue, or red fabric, with the finished design further enhanced by the addition of small circles or single 'petals' of other brightly coloured cloth – often silk – and *shisha*, the small pieces of mirror so typical of the embroideries of this region. A similar fold and cut technique is used to produce borders and other square or triangular motifs. The other style of *katab* is related, in that it also has as its starting point a square of fabric; this is cut into,

TOP LEFT: *Sample showing several variations of* katab *motifs. The bottom right-hand motif has been cut as one piece, India.*

TOP RIGHT: *Large basket covered with* katab *patterned cloth from Pakistan.*

producing a square of repeating cuts, which gives a pattern not unlike that of a fine stonework frieze; it has been suggested that the origin of this type of cutwork was inspired by the stone carvings on temple or mosque ceilings.

Katao

KATAO and *khatwa* are terms used further north, around New Delhi and the northern states. *Katao* is generally a simpler form, where the fabric is slashed in a series of straight cuts and the raw edges are turned under and stitched, producing a repeat pattern revealing the cloth beneath. *Khatwa* is a more figurative style, using shapes cut to represent animals, leaves, birds and figures. Animal trappings and the canopies for a cart (*maffa*) are often decorated with appliqué in this figurative style.

Other examples of appliqué from this region are the commercially produced hangings for wedding halls; they use the same fold and cut technique, but are constructed with the minimum amount of

stitching required to hold the various pieces together and are then liberally covered with sequins of different colours and sizes.

Orissan appliqué

ORISSAN appliqué from the east Indian state is another very distinctive, recognizable regional style, usually a white motif on bright primary coloured cloth. The shapes are cut from the cloth, in their finished size and shape – no allowance is made for a turned edge. The shape is stitched to the background fabric using chain stitch, often in white thread. Parrots, elephants and floral shapes are frequent motifs. The appliquéd item is often further enhanced by a central mandala of triangles of folded cloth arranged concentrically and rosettes of gathered cloth. Ric rac braid and gathered strips of cloth are also used. In the past this appliqué was employed almost solely for the decoration of canopies and huge umbrellas for processional and religious use, but today the technique is used to produce the usual array of smaller household items – cloths, cushions, small wall hangings – that find a ready sale to tourists.

OPPOSITE, BELOW; AND RIGHT: *Small container with* katab *appliqué used to line the interior, India; simple Egyptian appliquéd cushion panels like this are produced mainly for the tourist market, with the traditional lotus blossom design.*

EGYPTIAN APPLIQUÉ

THE craft of the tentmakers has been established in Old Cairo since the 9th century, in an area that was the gathering point for the caravan pilgrimages to Mecca, where great tents were erected to provide cool shelter. From the early part of the 17th century the area became known as the Street of the Tentmakers. Here in the open-fronted, cupboard-like workshops of this covered market, appliqué work is done by men. The designs are first drawn on paper and pricked with a needle, then dusted with charcoal powder to transfer the images to the background fabric. Appliqué pieces are cut as needed from a pile of coloured material, manipulated to fit the desired shape, and stitched down with the edges turned under.

The hangings developed from the embellishments of the great tents and their modern usage is not dissimilar – they decorate marquees for weddings, funerals, religious festivals and other important events and are also used to skirt the table of speakers at meetings and to provide an awning at the official opening of a new public building. They show scenes of local life, Pharaonic or folkloric subjects, geometric Islamic designs and decorative Arabic scripts. Larger tent hangings often include inscriptions bidding the guests welcome and a variation on the theme of 'Allah Bless this House'. Today, a panel of

ABOVE: *Orissan appliqué; the single colour motifs and white chain stitching used to attach them are typical of Orissan work from India.*

Arabic script could just as easily praise the artist's work, incorporating their name and telephone number. Local use of tentwork is increasingly threatened by the production of printed cottons that imitate the appliqué designs and are cheaper to produce. Other cloths have been developed: flags bearing the names of sheiks, covers for tombs of saints, cushion covers and wall hangings in softer colours with more tourist appeal

ABOVE: *Egyptian appliquéd cushion panel with arabesque scrolls.*

RIGHT: *Large hanging with geometric Islamic designs and Arabic scripts.*

and the Pharaonic scenes, reproduced in the early 20th century as a response to archaeological finds, are still popular today. The art of the Egyptian tentmaker is very much a part of a living tradition that continues to flourish and adapt to changing tastes.

BRODERIE PERSE

THREE

APPLIQUÉ

AN ancient technique that had been practised in the Middle Ages, Broderie Perse takes its name from its resemblance to Persian embroidery; it became popular during the 18th and 19th centuries in Britain and North America. The cutting out of motifs from printed fabrics and appliquéing them onto a plain cloth grew out of the necessity to extend the use of the brilliantly coloured chintz from India. Following the setting up of the East India Trading Company and the

ABOVE: *Patchwork quilt with a variation of the American patchwork block, Double Nine Patch, and Broderie Perse appliqué designs using a printed cotton fabric.*

RIGHT; AND DETAIL: *Patchwork, appliqué and quilted bed cover, 1819, made in East Yorkshire, England; the detail shows an appliquéd corner.*

importing of chintz fabrics, far brighter than anything available in Europe, embroideries were sent to India to be copied. The resulting fabrics were so sought after that a ban was placed on their import to help assuage the discontentment of fabric manufacturers in France and England. In 1721 a further law was passed banning the use of this imported fabric on any furniture, clothing or bed covers. This only served to encourage the frugal use of chintz fabrics and to salvage designs from old bed curtains and re-use them in appliqué. This technique was so popular in North America in the 19th century that chintz fabrics were especially designed for such a purpose. In order to help the cut-out designs keep their shape, the back of the design was coated in a paste. Once this was dry the motif could be positioned and stitched, but when the item was laundered, the paste would wash out. Finer details could be added with embroidery.

NARRATIVE QUILTS AND HANGINGS

Throughout the centuries the pictorial narrative technique has been used to tell a story, for instance, the medieval Tristan and Isolde quilt from Germany. The best-known story quilts are African-American, often depicting Biblical themes. Bible stories and religious symbols have inspired artists throughout the ages. In an era when not everyone could read, the stories heard in Church became the subjects for a number of quilts, such as Adam and Eve and Noah's Ark, often portrayed in the manner of colourful illustrations found in children's books.

Two of the best-known Bible quilts were made in North America by Harriet Powers, who was born a slave in Georgia in 1837. The portrayal of people and animals are similar to those found in West Africa on the flags of coastal Fante war companies and the heraldic banners of the kings of Dahomey. The quilts indicate a vast biblical knowledge and the influence of folklore and legend, with the addition of astronomical and seasonal occurrences. Through their narrative qualities they stand as two of North America's greatest figurative quilts.

ABOVE (AND DETAIL); AND OPPOSITE, ABOVE, LEFT: *Narrative hanging decorated with scenes from the story of Salur Masud, northern India; the detail shows an appliquéd scene;* khatwa, *a pictorial hanging, depicting scenes from village life, northern India.*

OPPOSITE, RIGHT: *An English collage of subjects studied at Goldsmiths College, London, in 1950. It was worked under the guidance of Constance Howard.*

OPPOSITE, BELOW: *Figurative French tablecloth, from Brittany, with domestic scenes.*

Pictorial or scenic quilts were first made in the 20th century, mostly in appliqué, and were highly detailed. The narrative Indian quilts, made in Bihar, portray the lives and culture of the women and their observations on local issues and the environment. In northern India, narrative cloths continue to be constructed; once made as offerings to be given at the shrine of Salar Masud, cruder, hastily made versions are now sold to tourists. In Peru and Colombia the hand-stitched, appliquéd hangings depict rural life, with three-dimensional imagery; they are embellished with embroidery.

THREE

APPLIQUÉ

REVERSE APPLIQUÉ

MOLA

THE word mola can mean cloth, clothing or blouse, although to most people it has come to signify the stitched panel made in the San Blas region of Panama by Kuna women. By the mid-1800s cloth, scissors and thread had been introduced and stimulated the development of needle-worked clothing.

Bright colours and intricate zoomorphic designs were not used until the early 1900s. It is thought that geometric patterns were employed before this date as borders and were painted either onto the skin or cloth. Stitched versions of

these painted designs appeared late in the 19th century.

The terms reverse appliqué and molas have frequently been combined, but traditional molas are made with various appliqué techniques, including overlay appliqué, inlay appliqué and a form of reverse appliqué. Most molas are made of two or three main layers of fabric, usually cotton, dyed in bright colours. The first two layers are laid on top of each other and

ABOVE: *Fragment showing an animal, possibly a dog, worked in a mola technique with three layers of cotton fabric.*

BELOW: *Mola, from Panama, with zoomorphic designs worked in a reverse appliqué technique. Extra details are worked in embroidery.*

OPPOSITE, ABOVE, LEFT: *Mola-type reverse appliqué, from Guatemala, with animated figures.*

THREE

APPLIQUÉ

LEFT: HOW TO CONSTRUCT A MOLA: EACH LAYER IS ADDED IN SUCCESSION; THE BLUE AND WHITE MOTIFS SHOW A COUNTERCHANGE TECHNIQUE.

the outline of the main design is cut down, through the top layer, and turned under and stitched to the next layer to form a channel. Subsequent layers can be added and subsequent cuttings will reveal the previous layer and also the layer below that. Small pieces of different fabrics can be slotted in between the layers so that when lines are cut to fill in a large area more colours will be seen when they are then turned back and stitched. Sometimes the base layer is put together in an inlay form with small pieces of fabric fitted

BELOW, LEFT; AND BELOW, RIGHT: *Three-coloured mola with geometric patterns; modern mola, made for the tourist market, mainly of cotton fabrics but with some man-made textiles. embroidery. – 3/3.*

RIGHT; AND DETAIL: *Hmong reverse appliqué, northern Thailand; the detail shows the minute turnings of the top fabric to create the scroll design.*

together like a jigsaw, which are revealed when the layer above it is cut back.

Inspiration for mola designs comes from everyday life: flora, fauna, myths, religious beliefs and rites of passage. The subjects of the molas are as diverse as the women who make them. Almost all Kuna women make molas, not as a pastime, but as a source of income. Despite the long hours spent in construction (they can take up to 100 hours to stitch), molas do not survive long in the hot and humid climate and with repeated washings.

The first Mola Cooperative was formed in the 1960s to unite artisans and promote their craft. The role of Kuna women has changed through the marketing of molas, which have become one of the most important products of the Kuna economy.

THAILAND

A NUMBER of hill-tribe peoples live in the mountain regions of northern and western Thailand. They migrated from China, in search of freedom and a land of their own, and settled in the upper mountain regions of what are now Laos, Thailand and north Vietnam.

There are six main groups, known in Thailand as the Karen, the Hmong, the Meo or Mien, the Akha, the Lisu and the Lahu, with the Karen being the largest tribal group. Each tribal group has their own beliefs and traditions, which govern their behaviour and the costume they wear. Red is a favourite colour, a powerful and protective colour. Triangles protect from the evil eye and stars, spirals, diamonds and waves are all ancient motifs, appearing as decorative elements in their costume. Designs may imitate nature and in the Hmong group zig zags represent centipedes, which are valued for their medicinal qualities. The centre of the spiral is thought to represent Hmong ancestors and the outer part successive generations. The Meo women make baby-

THREE

APPLIQUÉ

LEFT: *Single pennant for a toran of reverse appliqué; the red fabric has been cut back to reveal the white fabric beneath, Rajasthan, India.*

carrying cloths decorated with batik and appliqué as well as jackets with layers of appliqué on the sleeves. The Lisu women produce the most detailed clothes and they decorate their tunics with multi-coloured, tucked appliqué.

The reverse appliqué of the tribal groups from Thailand is often confused with the molas of the San Blas Indians of Panama. The designs both consist of channels of background fabric that show through cuts in an overlay fabric, but there the similarity ends. Molas are mainly pictorial in nature, while the reverse

appliqués of South-East Asia are geometric – either snowflake-like or as a single motif repeated over the entire design. In Hmong appliqué the design is generally precut into a multi-folded top layer before the layers are assembled, establishing lines of symmetry and a near perfect geometric pattern. Appliqué in the traditional dress of tribal groups in

TOP: *Hmong woman's jacket, decorated with expertly worked panels of reverse appliqué, Thailand.*

ABOVE; AND DETAIL: *Exceptionally finely worked appliqué jacket from the Hmong people of Thailand.*

RIGHT: *Hmong girl stitching a sample of reverse appliqué.*

THREE

APPLIQUÉ

southern China is closely related to the techniques and styles of the hill tribes in northern Thailand; some of the ethnic groups are culturally identical.

As large numbers of Thai Hmong have migrated to North America, this form of appliqué is known there and various aid agencies working within the poorer villages and refugee camps of northern

Thailand have sought to preserve and market the textile skills of the women, particularly *pa ndau* appliqué.

Today, factory-dyed black cloth tends to be used for the background instead of the indigo and a paler colour palette is chosen when producing cushion covers, bedspreads and bags for the tourist and export markets.

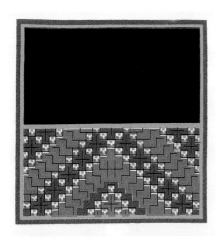

Opposite, left (and detail); opposite, right; and near right: *Hmong baby carrier showing the double coil design known as Elephant's Foot or Snailhouse, Thailand; detail showing the exquisitely worked reverse appliqué; strip from a Hmong woman's 'apron', Thailand, which is made from small squares of geometric reverse appliqué, highlighted with minute embroidery stitches; modern piece of reverse appliqué in a design very similar to printed cloth.*

Top left; and above, right: *Cloth printed with reverse appliqué designs, to replace the painstaking handwork, both from Thailand.*

Left; and top right: *Waist-coat, from southern China, with floral reverse appliqué panels; small panel of finely worked reverse appliqué, Thailand.*

161

Inlay appliqué

THE ORIGINS of inlay appliqué are to be found in Italy, Spain and the Middle East. It has been described as the technique that links true patchwork and appliqué. Where applied designs are cut and stitched onto a background fabric, inlay involves the setting in of patterns into a perfectly cut background. The two are frequently cut at the same time to ensure a perfect fit and both sides of the work are alike. The pieces are generally sewn together with a darning stitch or a fine oversewing stitch.

Europe

BY the 16th century in France, Italy and Spain leather or stiffened fabrics such as velvet or heavy brocade were being used for appliqué onto furnishings and saddle trappings using this technique. The fabrics were stiffened with glue and paper and inlaid into the background fabric and sewn with a cord couched around the edge.

During the late 18th and early 19th centuries the district of Azerbaijan was famous for overlaid and inlaid appliqué. Here, pieces of felt, woven wool or cotton fabric were applied to, or set into, a felt, woven wool or cotton ground. Resht, in Iran, was the city associated with this technique, where it was executed by both men and women. Floral designs and portraits of monarchs and other notables were worked, generally as wall hangings. Applied motifs were held in place with lines of tamboured chain stitch, worked in silk. Many of the best surviving examples are now in museums in western Europe.

Ghana

THIS technique re-emerged in the 19th century, when it was used to make banners and altar cloths from brocades and velvet with a couched gold cord, in the West. From 1850, when Ghana became a British colony, flags were being made, using the inlay technique, frequently out of trade cloth and recycled cloths, but also wool and silk.

THREE

APPLIQUÉ

Uniform Fabrics

Dᴜʀɪɴɢ the later part of the 19th century a particular type of inlay was being produced, mainly in Britain and almost exclusively by tailors. It was made from heavy, non-fraying uniform or suit cloth, embellished with embroidery and was mainly figurative. Each piece usually had a chain stitch outline or was couched over a gold cord, and resembled marquetry. This technique demanded a high degree of skill and artistry. The same uniform fabrics were also being used to produce the geometric patchwork of the soldier's quilts.

Oᴘᴘᴏsɪᴛᴇ, ᴛᴏᴘ; ᴀɴᴅ ᴏᴘᴘᴏsɪᴛᴇ, ʙᴇʟᴏᴡ (ᴀɴᴅ ᴅᴇᴛᴀɪʟ): *Wool-felt inlay with the appearance of a series of tiles, Turkey; piece of Resht work on a fine woven wool ground, with a complex floral design; the detail shows the central panel from the reverse side, revealing the intricate construction.*

Aʙᴏᴠᴇ; ᴀɴᴅ ʀɪɢʜᴛ: *Inlay figurative hanging made from soldiers' and sailors' uniform material, with additional embroidery, England, 19th century; detail from a flag made by the Fante people of West Africa, with warriors worked using the inlay technique in cotton fabric.*

PATCHWORK

GEOMETRIC
PATCHWORK
AMERICAN BLOCK
STRIP PATCHWORK
FREEFORM PATCHWORK
FOLDED AND OTHER
3-D PATCHWORK FORMS

Geometric patchwork

The technique of sewing scraps of a textile together to create a fabric is an ancient one, but because of the perishable nature of material, very little patchwork dating back more than a few centuries has survived. Archaeologists in China in the 1920s found a collection of ancient, pieced, silk and damask items in the Caves of the Thousand Buddhas, along the Silk Road, which are believed to date from the 8th century. Among the finds was a multi-coloured, votive hanging made from patched triangles and rectangles, and several pieces of mosaic patchwork. The patches were joined together by oversewing on the wrong side of the fabric, demonstrating that true patchwork, in construction and appearance, has remained unchanged for over a thousand years.

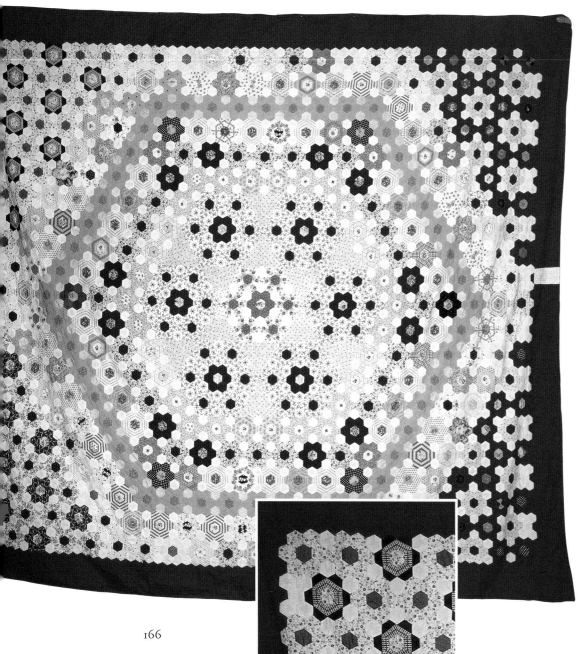

Italy

During an air raid on Italy in 1944, the Church of Impruneta, near Florence, was bombed and the sepulchre of the Bishop Antonio Bellincione degli Agli was damaged. During the restoration of the sepulchre, a pillow that had been placed under the Bishop's head was discovered; it was made some time before 1477. Two different designs make up the front and back of the cushion; small diamond shapes have been pieced on one side and eight-pointed stars set with squares and triangles to create circles have been pieced on the other side. These popular geometric designs can be seen in the mosaic floors in Romanesque churches. The materials were joined together with coloured threads using a cording stitch. Very little medieval patchwork has survived, but similar designs and a similar technique can be seen on 18th-century Swedish wedding cushions. The Italian cushion is proof that patchwork was a domestic pastime.

England and France

In the 18th century restrictions on the importing of Indian cottons and chintz in England and France meant that fabrics were regarded as precious. When patterned material was scarce and lengths of fabric difficult to obtain, every piece of

TOP LEFT; AND ABOVE, LEFT (DETAIL): *Patchwork of extremely small hexagons expertly sewn together to create a star shape, 19th century; detail of the hexagon rosettes.*

ABOVE; AND DETAIL: *Design showing concentric hexagons creating a stunning pattern in dress-weight silks, 19th century; detail highlighting the richness of the silk fabrics used.*

OPPOSITE, ABOVE, RIGHT: *Equilateral triangles of bark cloth that formed part of a ceremonial skirt from West Africa; in Europe one form of this pattern was known as Pharaoh's Pyramids.*

OPPOSITE, LEFT; AND DETAIL: *The hexagon was one of the most popular of geometric patchwork shapes, worked over papers; the angles formed were shallow, making it easy to sew together and achieve a good result. The detail shows the hexagon rosettes.*

cloth had to be made to go further. Plain fabrics and the precious printed materials were pieced together to form larger cloths required for quilts and bed curtains. A complete set of bed furnishings (curtains, pelmets, valances and a quilted bedspread), thought to have been made in 1708, has survived in the north of England, at Levens Hall in Cumbria. The fabrics have been pieced together, using hexagons, crosses, octagons and diamonds.

Technique

THE technique most often seen in early patchwork has come to be called 'English Patchwork' and the most common shape was the hexagon. Paper templates were cut to create the shape and the fabric pieces were tacked over the templates, which were then oversewn together. Small, intricate, tessellating patterns, known as mosaic patchwork, can be constructed in this way. One such pattern, the box or cube, known in patchwork as Tumbling Blocks

THREE

PATCHWORK

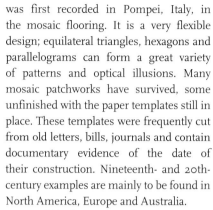

was first recorded in Pompei, Italy, in the mosaic flooring. It is a very flexible design; equilateral triangles, hexagons and parallelograms can form a great variety of patterns and optical illusions. Many mosaic patchworks have survived, some unfinished with the paper templates still in place. These templates were frequently cut from old letters, bills, journals and contain documentary evidence of the date of their construction. Nineteenth- and 20th-century examples are mainly to be found in North America, Europe and Australia.

Pieced block patterns, of similar designs to the American block patchwork, were made in England in the early 19th century using this method, rather than the more practical American method of seaming. These were less common than Medallion

THREE

PATCHWORK

OPPOSITE, FAR LEFT;
OPPOSITE, ABOVE, RIGHT (AND
DETAIL); AND OPPOSITE, BELOW:
*Diamond shape, sewn over papers, where the play
of light and dark fabrics create a design known
as Tumbling Blocks; cloth, from Turkestan, with
a patchwork border of plain and patterned cloth
surrounding a simply pieced centre; child's
patchwork cot quilt, with* katab *appliqué, India.*

ABOVE, LEFT; AND ABOVE,
RIGHT: *Baby carrier, from Burma, with
an embroidered and appliquéd centre panel
placed on patchwork cloth of half square triangles;
Siberian Samoyed family – their clothing is pieced
from differently coloured furs.*

BELOW: *Detail of a* tivaivai *quilt, pieced or* taorei,
characteristic of Tahiti and the Cook Islands.

quilts, or Frame quilts, which could contain as many as ten borders, pieced from plain and patterned fabrics. There are many surviving examples of geometric, pieced patchwork, made by men, generally soldiers, using uniform fabric.

Pakistan

IN the late 19th century Sudanese 'dervish' warriors and their horses still displayed the pieced and quilted armour that could be traced back to at least the 12th century. These were made of a cotton cloth in primary colours and their patterns influenced the heraldic images seen on medieval armour in Europe. The patterns favoured are often squares and triangles and very much like the patchwork of Sind, Pakistan, hundreds of miles to the north-east. It is thought that the style travelled by the trade routes. Patterns worked on the patchwork *rallis*, the quilts of Pakistan and

north-west India, are designs made from squares and triangles, typically in a limited palette of red, green, black, white and yellow, and can be traced back to designs on ancient pottery. These patchwork quilt tops are then layered with a thin wadding, often an old quilt or old fabric, and then quilted.

Central Asia

IN Central Asia, patchwork is used for both horse and camel trappings, and for household items. The fabrics used and the design arrangement and techniques can be seen as evidence of contact between peoples from as far apart as north-east Iran and the Sudan. Each motif is made up of a series of coloured rectangular or diamond-shaped pieces, sewn in lines to form triangular sections, which are then joined together to reveal the overall pattern. Flowers are often featured as a motif, but as a symbolic representation.

AMERICAN BLOCK

I T IS generally accepted that quiltmaking skills were brought to North America by European settlers. Only a few surviving American quilts pre-date 1830 and although there is documentary evidence of quilts dating from the 17th and 18th centuries, there is no certainty that they were actually made in North America. In all probability, the American block quilt was born in the early 19th century. Blocks, as units, were always a convenient method of piecing when space was limited and American quilters took to the idea of repeating blocks and a huge variety of patterns, both pieced and appliquéd, developed.

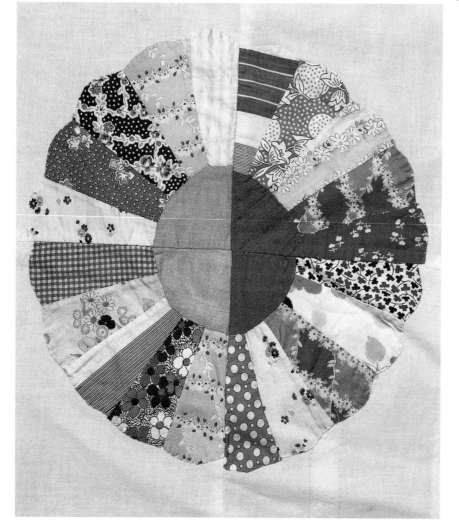

The Pioneers

P IONEER women in North America frequently kept a record of new patterns they saw, by making up a single block. These collections were considered to be valuable and were often mentioned in wills; they are a visual history of the textiles either brought to the American West from the eastern United States and Europe, or produced locally within the territory. They contain clues as to the textiles, dyes and resources available and provide background information on the owners' place of origin. They are a true history of European-American quilts during the 19th and early 20th centuries.

Quilts made in Europe after 1850 show distinct American influence in both the design and the style of piecing. There is evidence that this transatlantic exchange of ideas also worked in reverse and it is now generally accepted that the American Amish learnt their quilting in the New World from their 'English' neighbours who were originally from Wales and northern England, as is evident in the strong colours and designs and the flowing quilting patterns they used. This exchange of ideas was strengthened in magazines such as *Godey's Lady's Book*. In the 20th century, the making of quilts

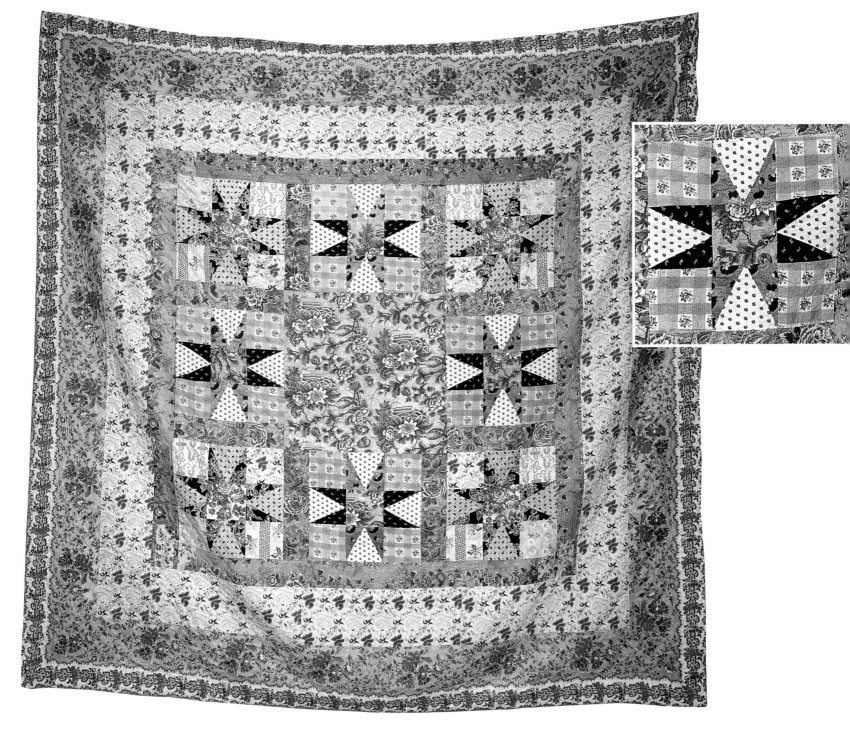

in North America was formalized when printed patterns started to appear in books and magazines and were also available by mail order. Fabric companies such as Sears and Roebuck started to produce quilt designs in kit form; the Dresden Plate design, in 1890, was one such kit.

The quilt patterns developed by the pioneer women reflected their day-to-day lives; the gardens they created, the places they passed through, the sky and the sea, battles that were fought, stories that were told. 'Burgoyne Surrounded' commemorates the surrender of General Burgoyne at the Battle of Saratoga in 1777, one of the most important events in the lead up to American Independence. Generations of American women kept history and traditions alive and preserved in the quilt blocks that were sewn and passed on to friends and family. As they moved through the country, the names of old block designs changed to reflect new surroundings. Many old patterns had different names at different times and in different parts of the country. Bear Paw is one such pattern, called The Hand of Friendship by the Quakers, Bear Tracks

OPPOSITE, FAR LEFT; OPPOSITE, ABOVE; OPPOSITE, BELOW: *American patchwork blocks, from the top: Five patch Basket block, Nine patch Star block, Nine patch Churn Dash or Monkey Wrench block, Four patch Flower Basket block, Simple Signature block; printed cotton fabrics cut and sewn together in multiples of six pieces prior to making up into a quilt, North America; American block patchwork – the Dresden Plate design which was marketed in kit form from the 1890s.*

ABOVE; AND DETAIL: *American quilt with eight multiples of the same star block design and surrounding borders of printed cotton, 20th century.*

THREE

PATCHWORK

in Ohio and Duck's Foot in the Mud in New York. Conversely, the same name may be applied to several different block patterns. Literature inspired blocks such as Delectable Mountains from John Bunyan's *Pilgrim's Progress* and The Lady of the Lake was created to honour the tales of Sir Walter Scott.

Various block techniques

QUILT blocks were put together to create all-over repeating designs, but this is not the only way in which they can be sewn. Sampler quilts were a collection of many different blocks, generally made by one person and frequently used as a way of learning and recording new designs. Album quilts, popular in the 19th century, were a communal project, combining patchwork and appliqué techniques, often to commemorate a special event. Friendship quilts were also communal, signed, Sampler quilts, made for a friend or relative who was moving away. A Freedom quilt was an Album quilt with signed blocks, made for a young man reaching the age

ABOVE, LEFT; ABOVE, RIGHT; AND LEFT: *Amish Star within a Star, North America; North Country quilt with the Sanderson Star, England; American block patchwork designs: Basket block and Star block, arranged as a central panel in a frame quilt, with plain and pieced borders.*

OPPOSITE, BELOW, LEFT; AND OPPOSITE, BELOW, RIGHT: *Single Irish Chain quilt design; Triple Irish Chain design made by Gene Bowen – a variation on Irish Chain.*

THREE

PATCHWORK

of twenty-one, generally by female relatives and friends. Similar to this was the Autograph or Signature quilt, a communal quilt often incorporating a block with an open space in the centre, large enough to embroider a signature or verse. These were sometimes used as fundraisers, with the name of a church or charity incorporated. Within this range of quilts can be found the Red Cross quilts, made in 1917 and 1918; some as fundraisers, others simply a means of warmth for soldiers or anyone to whom the Red Cross gave comfort.

Quilts can be seen as being visual records of women's lives and the quilt blocks of North America tell its history. Group quilts can contribute much to the development of the social concerns and economic issues of a community.

ABOVE: *Amish Bars quilt design attributed to the Pennsylvania Amish of Lancaster County, however, it may have its roots in the English quiltmaking tradition of North Country strippy quilt designs.*

STRIP PATCHWORK

SEMINOLE

THE Seminole and Miccosukee peoples of Florida in North America are descended from the Creek Nation, who, it is believed, can trace their ancestry to the Mayan Indians of South America. In 1821 Florida officially came under the control of the United States; by 1858, after the three Seminole Wars, the nation had dwindled to several hundred indigenous peoples and an unknown number of descendants of former runaway African slaves.

In 1880 government agents found these now small tribal groups. Trading posts were established and the tribal groups traded alligator skins and bird plumes for cloth, needles, beads, food staples and metal tools. The traders' wives taught basic sewing techniques, but it was the introduction of the sewing machine that caught the creative imagination of the Seminole women and transformed Seminole dress. The traders also introduced bias tape, fancy edging and ric rac trims, which were incorporated into the Seminole garments.

The Seminoles' characteristic structural patchwork, made by joining torn strips of cloth lengthwise into long, multi-coloured bands, cutting these bands into segments and assembling them in a pre-planned order into long bands of geometric pattern, developed at a time when most other elements of their traditional culture had been lost. While the Seminoles were not the first to use the strip method of piecing, they were the first to carry through the design possibilities in their work. New fabric was always used and the clothing was never quilted. Early documented rows of patchwork designs appear in photographs of families who came to live in Seminole exhibition villages. These villages became a refuge for many families. The pieced clothing was the creation of the Miccosukee-speaking Indian women.

By the 1930s this form of patchwork was also being made for the tourist trade. Their colourful clothing is the most visible art form of the Seminole culture.

THREE

PATCHWORK

ABOVE, LEFT: *The stages in the construction of a Seminole pattern.*

TOP RIGHT: *Cushion with Seminole patchwork created from strips of cotton fabric, North America.*

RIGHT: *Typical skirt of the Seminole women of North America constructed from bands of patterns, separated with plain strips, mid-20th century.*

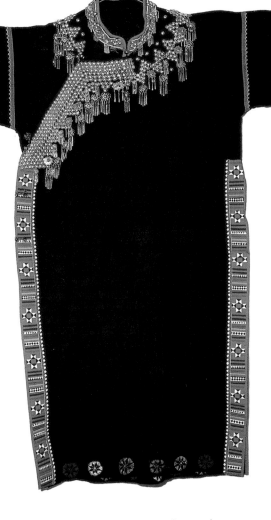

ABOVE: *Lahu woman's coat, from northern Thailand; the edges are decorated with expertly worked strips of folded patchwork.*

LEFT; AND ABOVE: *Persian woman with strip decoration on her short jacket, 19th century; North Country strippy quilt, heavily quilted, with the quilting patterns following the fabric strips, England.*

RIGHT: *Group of Russian women, their full skirts decorated with many contrasting strips.*

FREEFORM PATCHWORK

AFRICAN-AMERICAN PATCHWORK

IMPROVISATION is a prominent charact-eristic of African-American quilts; many African textile artists and African-American quiltmakers use traditional patterns and styles as the basis for their work, but new forms occur spontaneously. African values favour individuality and encourage the unexpected and the unique. African-American quiltmakers enjoy the unplanned element and piecing is seen as a process in which interesting things can happen. 'Mistakes' may be acceptable, or not seen as mistakes at all, but an integral part of the creative process.

African-American quiltmaking emerged in a context of poverty where recycling cloth made good sense. Quilts were created from scraps of fabric and in order to get the most out of these scraps they were sometimes simply sewn together. These were Utility quilts, meant for everyday use.

Exciting quilts result from bringing together existing quilting designs, but using approximately measured piecing and accommodating any accidental variations that may emerge. In the Anglo-traditional quilt the overall appearance is predeter-mined by the fabric and the pattern. Afro-traditional piecing must continually make adjustments since by using approxi-mate measurements each block may be a different size and shape. Having to deal with irregularities as they occur allows for the process of improvisation – a quilt layout is adapted to fit the available pieces.

Strip or string piecing, where strips of different lengths may be utilized, are especially popular in the African tradition since they are an efficient way of using up material. Anglo-traditional patterns favour the repeat of the single motif but, in contrast to this, the improvisational approach provides a range of possible structures, which will not repeat, but can be continually modified.

Another African-American improvisa-tional technique involves the restructuring of an existing quilt by cutting it up and putting it back together in a new way. This allows the quiltmaker to redo a design; to add in found, inherited or leftover patchwork pieces or to assemble a quilt top from a range of differently sized blocks. If a block does not fit a particular space, it may be added to or cut down. Oversized blocks can be cut up and reworked to form the basis for yet more improvisations.

THREE

PATCHWORK

CRAZY PATCHWORK

CRAZY patchwork has its origins in various cultures, but reached the height of its popularity in the 19th century. Few examples exist prior to 1830, but it is thought that asymmetrical Japanese designs influenced the late Victorian development of crazy patchwork in the West. It is known that during the 1830s, in Japan, women made clothing and household items using a technique known as *yosegire* which was a means of extending

the life of special fabrics when they were scarce. Pieced coats and kimonos were put together using strips of crazy-type patches. In 1876 the Japanese stand at the Centennial Exposition in Philadelphia exhibited a range of textiles with oddly cut, crazy patchwork and this inspired the needlewomen of the day.

RIGHT: *Crazy patchwork cushion embellished mainly with feather stitch; it uses knitted synthetic fabrics as well as the more usual cotton and silks.*

OPPOSITE: *A haphazard arrangement of fabrics within each block creates a lively feeling of movement within this African-American quilt, early 20th century.*

RIGHT; AND DETAIL: *Cover for the headboard of a bed using printed cotton fabrics in a crazy patchwork manner.*

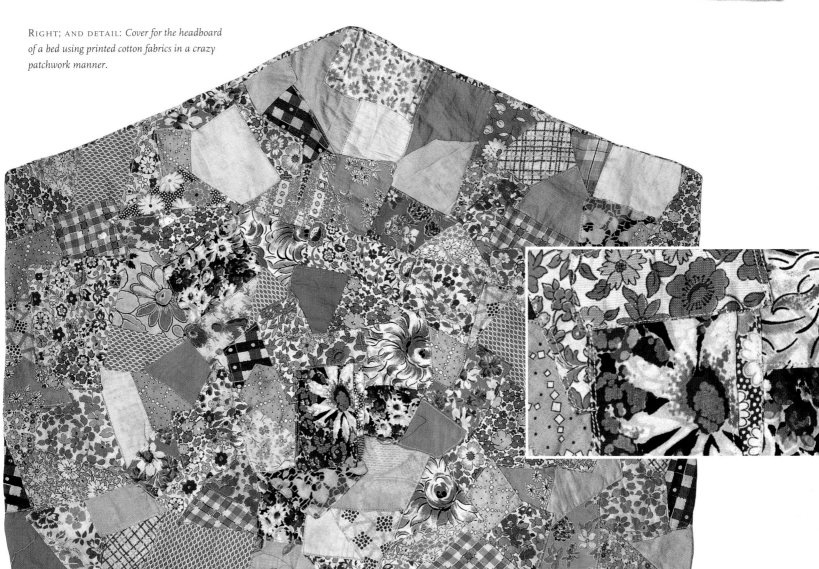

THREE

PATCHWORK

Crazy patchwork in the West

I N the West prior to the 19th century crazy patchwork was a thrift craft and the product of poverty. Many different fabrics – wool, flannel, cotton and linen – would be combined to make a quilt that was entirely utilitarian, simply a means of keeping warm and, not surprisingly, very few examples have survived.

In the second half of the 19th century crazy or puzzle patchwork was very popular on both sides of the Atlantic and in Australia. *Godey's Lady's Book*, one of the first women's magazines to be published in North America, advertised mail order kits for crazy patchwork in 1885. Crazy patchwork filled the demand for needlework which was simply done, but rich and showy. It became a popular activity for genteel ladies with time on their hands. The patchwork was constructed by stitching random patches to a fabric base; incorporating snippets of velvets, brocades, silks and satins from the clothing of the time and the fancy braids and ribbons that were available to the more affluent members of society. It frequently became an excuse to try out all the embroidery stitches, to use silk embroidery threads and to incorporate beads and sequins; patches of plain materials were embroidered with complex designs. The resulting patchworks were

OPPOSITE (AND DETAIL); AND ABOVE, LEFT: *Crazy patchwork was popular on both sides of the Atlantic and in Australia in the second half of the 19th century; distorted squares, rectangles and triangles are a design feature of* pojagi, *wrapping cloths, from Korea.*

a riot of colour, not necessarily done in the best of taste. They were made into bed coverings, cushions, covers for furniture, including pianos, and all manner of household items from tea cosies to book covers and smoking caps. They were frequently signed or initialled and nearly always dated.

Crazy patchwork is still being produced today, but the format has changed and there are many varieties of this freeform technique, from crazy Log Cabin to crazy strip patchwork.

Traditional Korean patchwork

IN previous centuries Korean women lived in a male-dominated society and did not receive any formal education, but concentrated on domestic tasks such as weaving and embroidery, creating exquisite wrapping cloths and covers by collecting scraps of fabric left over from making dresses and quilts. This technique was called *pojagi*.

POJAGI PATCHWORK

POJAGI cloths are both functional and beautiful, made from scraps of material ranging from cotton, ramie, hemp, silk and paper; wonderful combinations of colour, pattern and texture are common features of these utilitarian cloths. *Chog'akpo* is a variant of *pojagi* using both old and new cloth, and often heavier fabrics than the traditional sheer materials. Traditional cloths show the symbolic use of the five colours associated with *ying-yang*: blue, yellow, red, white and black. The patches are joined into squares and the square form extended until the cloth reaches the required size. The *chog'akpo* are constructed using long, wide, distorted and regular squares and triangles, pieced together in a pleasing arrangement. No two are alike; all maintain an individuality. Seams play a large role in the design and

TOP CENTRE; TOP RIGHT; AND ABOVE: *A combination of old and new cloth is used to create these beautiful* pojagi, *wrapping cloths, from Korea. The use of blue, yellow, red, white and black colours are associated with* ying-yang; *unlike other patchwork techniques, the seams in* pojagi *play an important role in the design of the finished cloth.*

are emphasized instead of being hidden; they are also a distinguishing feature of *pojagi*. *Gekki* is the Korean term for a triple stitching technique, which frames each individual panel.

FOLDED AND OTHER 3-D PATCHWORK FORMS

Folded forms of patchwork are used to decorate both garments and quilts. Folded ribbon, tape, or lengths of rouleau, forming a mitred point, have often been used for decorative fastenings. Edges of garments, quilts and cushions are sometimes decorated using folded squares of fabric to create a saw-tooth edge or *prairie points*. The Lisu, a hill tribe from Thailand, create bands of narrow strips and tiny folded patches, which are applied to garments and bags. In Orissa, eastern India, three-dimensional folded triangles are used with the traditional appliqué. In North America, in the 1890s, there was a brief fashion for 'Quill' patchwork. Folded Star or Mitred patchwork, another decorative folded form, is thought to have developed in Canada; a form of it was recorded in North America in 1850 and in the 1970s, in Britain, it became known as Somerset patchwork.

Cathedral Window

As a patchwork, Cathedral Window is unlike any other form. Far from being 'born of thrift', Cathedral Window requires four times its area in the folded squares, so it is quite wasteful of fabric and the resulting piece of work is heavy. It is not certain where it originated. One theory is that it began in North America at the turn of the 20th century, but the motif

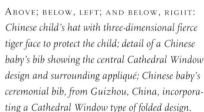

has been used traditionally on children's clothing and baby carriers in China, where it symbolized prosperity and was used to ward off the evil eye. The technique is also seen in examples of the Korean patchwork, *pojagi*, and it is thought to have partly originated from origami, the Japanese art of paper folding. The basic shape requires two folded squares of background fabric plus one smaller square

ABOVE; BELOW, LEFT; AND BELOW, RIGHT: *Chinese child's hat with three-dimensional fierce tiger face to protect the child; detail of a Chinese baby's bib showing the central Cathedral Window design and surrounding appliqué; Chinese baby's ceremonial bib, from Guizhou, China, incorporating a Cathedral Window type of folded design.*

LEFT: *Chinese baby carrier with folded patchwork flower-like designs on either side.*

ABOVE: *Panel created by the Lisu tribe of Thailand; constructed from narrow strips of cotton fabric with inserts of tiny folded triangles.*

ABOVE: ROSETTE OF SMALL SUFFOLK PUFFS.

for the window. The background squares are folded and re-folded, to create double 'envelopes', which are oversewn together, and the smaller 'window' square is placed over the join. The top folds of the envelope are rolled over the edges of the window and sewn down onto it, creating the effect of a four-petalled flower.

Suffolk Puffs

SUFFOLK Puffs, also known as Rosettes, Bon-Bons and Yo-Yos, are a fragile three-dimensional patchwork form, often made from scraps of dress cotton and shirting, and mainly found in Britain, Canada, Australia and North America. Samples have survived from the 1890s,

and also from the 1920s and 1930s, at the height of its popularity; but it was never the most popular method of patchwork. Individual puff pieces are made from a circle of fabric, with the edge turned in, then gathered up and flattened out. They are sewn to each other by oversewing to the next puff with a few stitches.

COLLECTING AND CARE OF TEXTILES

IT is possible to collect at random – any textile that captures the eye – but a collection will benefit from having a theme or focus. For instance, collecting many examples of a particular object – such as hats or wallhangings – or from a certain country or region, or a particular technique – pieced patchwork, for example.

Collecting may be, but does not have to be, expensive, since smaller or contemporary pieces can be just as desirable and interesting as fine, old examples. Pieces are generally less expensive if bought in the country of origin, but this is of course offset by the cost of travel; the knowledge gained from examining pieces in their cultural context is, however, invaluable. Other collectors, textile dealers and specialist galleries are all good sources of information and most are more than willing to share their knowledge.

Keep a record of where and when each piece was bought, how much was paid for it and as much other information as possible, especially if bought in the country of origin. Make a note of any local name for the piece or the technique and also what the item was used for. When researching a piece, keep an open mind, since some pieces may be wrongly attributed. For instance, a piece described as 'African mirror work', while bought in South Africa, was in fact of Gujarati origin – a large Gujarati community lives in South Africa.

As the collection increases in size, display, storage and possibly cleaning become important considerations.

DISPLAY

BOTH display and storage have some points in common; for instance, both direct sunlight and fluorescent tube lighting will damage textiles, whether on display or in storage. Strong spotlights trained on fabric will cause damage due to heat and will also attract dust; excessive dryness, heat or damp, and moths can cause fibres to weaken and rot.

Hanging quilts and wallhangings can cause some deterioration and can weaken the fibres, so do not leave them hanging for too long; rotate the items you have on show. If the object is large, heavy or difficult to display – this is often true of items of costume – this needs to be considered when selecting the item for display and deciding on the means of displaying it.

STORAGE

WHEN storing textiles, plastic bags are to be avoided, as moisture can be trapped inside the bag, leading to mildew.

If textiles are stored on unfinished wood or particle board shelving then the acids from the wood can discolour and weaken the fibres. This will not happen if the wood is painted with a polyurethane finish and shelves can be lined with aluminium foil or acid-free tissue paper for further protection. Glass doors in front of the shelves or a curtain or blind attached to the top shelf will keep dust and light away from your textile collection.

The storage of quilts and other large items may be governed by the amount of available space. Ideally this space should have an even temperature and have blinds at the windows to reduce light. The best way to store an object is to lay it out flat, but the alternative is to fold or roll it. When folding, the quilt should be folded top side out with rolls of acid-free tissue paper placed along the fold line and then placed in a cotton sheet or pillow case, or a box lined with acid-free tissue paper. The folded object should be taken out and refolded in a different way several times a year to prevent any permanent marking.

Quilts and hangings can be rolled around a cardboard tube covered with acid-free tissue paper, or a length of plastic drainpipe covered in cotton wadding. Before rolling, the quilt or hanging should be laid on top of a sheet and covered with a second sheet. Once rolled these can be tied, not too tightly, at intervals before covering with a further sheet that should also be tied.

If you have several quilts to store, do not stack them in a pile of more than about three as the weight will cause additional creasing.

All stored textiles benefit from being opened up and aired every six months, or at least once a year. The wrapping materials can be washed or replaced, and the textiles examined carefully for any signs of moths. If you suspect moths, seek professional advice, sooner rather than later. If you have a problem with moths in woollen cloth, the textile can be placed in a freezer for several months.

Avoid storing textiles around smokers since cigarette smoke soaks very quickly into a textile and this can cause colour changes and the deterioration of the fibres.

CLEANING TEXTILES

WHILE some textiles can be very successfully laundered, err on the side of caution and seek professional advice, preferably from a textile conservator, who will understand and be familiar with the particular difficulties presented by old textiles, rather than a high-street dry cleaner. Not only are old, worn textiles fragile, but also the dye colours may not be colourfast, or some fabrics may have finishes that will be damaged by washing. Wool or felt may shrink, and anything with fur, hide, skin, or leather should not be washed.

Nevertheless, soil trapped in fibres can often cause more damage than the laundering process. Careful, professional cleaning will lengthen the life of your textile. If you wish to attempt this yourself, then try to determine the colourfastness of each separate piece of fabric used. Gently rub a white cloth over each fabric to see if any colour rubs off, or apply a small piece of damp cotton wool to the fabric. Water temperature can affect the fabric's ability to retain its colour, so if the water is cold to tepid this will work best to ensure that the dye does not run. Chlorine can also cause some dyes to release their colour, so if you know your water supply is chlorinated, proceed with caution. Choose a safe, very mild, washing agent to clean your textiles. If the item you are laundering is large, either wash by hand and spin on a gentle spin cycle in the washing machine, or wash on a gentle wash cycle by machine; though even the gentlest of 'delicates' machine programmes give any old textile quite a battering; any laundering should only be attempted if you are certain that the piece can tolerate it.

Do not put a wet textile in a clothes' dryer – dry it flat out of doors. The item can be placed on top of a sheet and covered with a further sheet, to protect it from insects and the sun. If you have a large bush in your garden use it to dry the textile flat – it will give support and allow air circulation.

Gentle vacuuming can remove dust particles; it should be done over a fibreglass screening to protect the object. If there are loose pieces – bits of ribbon or beads, for instance – do so with caution.

Do not use a commercial cleaning product – if you wish to have a textile dry cleaned then choose a specialist cleaner who knows about textiles or a textile conservationist. It may work best simply to freshen up your textile by airing it out of doors when there is a light breeze.

GLOSSARY

abla *see shisha*

abr *see ikat*

adjective dye A dyestuff that needs a mordant to make it permanent

African-American patchwork A patchwork where the main characteristic is improvisation

AIDS quilt Personal and political banner to commemorate the death of an AIDS victim, often incorporating pieces of their clothing

Album quilt Quilt made from pieced and appliquéd blocks, with different designs made by different people as a commemoration or celebration

Amish A non-conformist people who are renowned for their plain clothing and do not use most modern devices. They mainly live in North America and Canada

aniline dyes Chemical or synthetic dyes originally derived from coal tar

appliqué Decorative technique of applying one piece of fabric to another

arpilleras Small panels depicting everyday life; they are peopled with small figures as an 'appliqué of protest' to mark the name of the 'disappeared' from Chile in the 1970s

Asafo flags Military company appliquéd flags of the Fante tribes of coastal Ghana

Autograph quilt Quilt made up of signed blocks

Baltimore Album quilt Intricate appliqué designs of baskets and flowers made up in block form

Banjara A once nomadic people, originally from Rajasthan in north-western India, who have now settled mostly in central and southern India

bas-relief *see trapunto*

batik The Javanese method of resist-dyeing with wax

batting American term for filling or wadding

Bible quilt Story quilt based on biblical tales

block patchwork Unit of patchwork, usually a square, that is a complete design within itself

block print Fabric that has been hand printed using wooden printing blocks

boro Japanese textiles reworked using patchwork, mending and stitching

brocade A figured fabric with a design developed by floating certain threads; used in furnishings

Broderie Perse Technique involving cutting out printed motifs and applying them to another fabric

calico Unbleached cotton cloth; called muslin in North America

Cathedral Window A folded fabric design with neither wadding nor backing fabric

chakla Square wallhanging, often made in pairs, found in India

Charm quilt A quilt in which no two pieces of fabric are the same

chasuble Sleeveless mantle worn by a priest

chintz Block printed and/or hand painted cotton fabric from India

corded quilting Technique in which closely spaced parallel lines are stitched and inserted with cotton or wool cord from the back; *see also* Italian quilting

crazy patchwork Randomly shaped patches stitched together, often embellished with embroidery stitches

damask A figured fabric in which warp satin and weft sateen weaves interchange; originally from the Syrian city of Damascus

dharaniyo Indian cover for stacked, folded bedding

doublet Man's waist-length, padded garment of silk, satin, velvet or leather

dye A colouring agent for cloth or yarn

Egyptian appliqué Hangings with appliqué designs made in the Street of the Tentmakers in Cairo

English patchwork Patchwork technique in which the fabric patches are basted over paper templates before being stitched to each other

felt A textile in which the fibres are densely matted

flat quilting Quilting the top and bottom layers of a quilt that has no wadding

flax Fibre used in linen fabrics

Folded Star patchwork (also Mitred patchwork) A decorative folded form, thought to have developed in Canada

Frame quilt Term used to describe British patchwork quilt layout in which the square centre is surrounded by a series of borders

Freedom quilt An Album quilt, of signed blocks, made for a young man on reaching the age of twenty-one; generally made by female friends and relatives

Friendship quilt Communal, signed sampler quilt for a friend or relative moving away

fustian The word comes from the Arabic meaning a heavy cotton cloth, but is often combined with linen as a linen warp and a cotton weft

futon Japanese traditional wadded sleeping mat

ger (also *yurt*) Round felt tent found in Central Asia and Mongolia

giveaways Ceremony unique to American Native communities in the Plains region, where many quilts are given as gifts

Hawaiian appliqué One-piece appliqué like a cut-out snowflake; applied to a background

hexagon The most common geometric shape used in English patchwork

Hmong People from the hills in Thailand who produce a form of geometric reverse appliqué

ikat Woven fabric in which the yarn is tied and dyed in a design before weaving

indigo One of the oldest dyestuffs known

inlay The technique that links true patchwork and appliqué, inlay involves the setting of a pattern into a perfectly cut background

Italian quilting Another term for corded quilting

jack An early kind of quilted armour with two outer fabric layers and plates of metal or horn enclosed within the padding

kanbiri A stitch used to form geometric quilted patterns in north-west India and Pakistan

kantha Quilted and embroidered cloths made from recycled fabric in West Bengal and Bangladesh

katab Appliqué work from north-west India, often produced by folding and cutting into the fabric

katao or **khatwa** Appliqué from northern India

linsey-woolsey Fabric with a linen warp and a woollen weft

Log Cabin Traditional patchwork block in which strips are sewn around a central square, with light strips on two sides and dark strips on the other two sides

madder The dried and ground-up roots of the madder plant produce many shades of red dye

Marcella quilt Machine-made, all-white quilt with a raised design that resembles trapunto

Marriage quilt Elaborate bridal quilt decorated with hearts, flowers and doves

mashru or **misru** A fabric, usually striped, that was originally a mix of silk and cotton; made in India for the Arabian market

Medallion quilt A series of pieced borders, arranged concentrically around a central design or medallion; also called Frame quilt

Memorial quilt Made from pieces of clothing belonging to someone who has died, incorporating the dates of their birth and death; also known as a Mourning quilt

mercerisation The process of using caustic soda to produce a more lustrous finish to cotton fibre; discovered by John Mercer

Mingei Japanese folk art

mola A stitched panel of reverse appliqué, frequently of intricate zoomorphic designs, made by the women of the Kuna people of the San Blas Islands off Panama

mordant A metallic salt that combines chemically with dyestuff to fix the dye

mosaic patchwork All-over geometric design that looks like a mosaic tiled floor

Mourning quilt Made to mark the death of a member of the family

Narrative quilt A quilt that tells a story

palampore Hindi and Persian name for a printed and painted cotton bedspread

pa ndau Flower cloth: reverse appliqué designs produced by the Hmong peoples from Thailand

pantoran Small wallhanging found in north-west India

patchwork Constructing a textile by sewing together small pieces of fabric into a geometric design

piecing Term used in North America for patchwork

pojagi A Korean wrapping cloth

Queen Anne quilting Flat quilting worked with yellow silk thread and a back stitch

quilting The stitching holding the layers of a quilt together

ralli A North Indian or Pakistani quilt

Red Cross quilts Quilts made as fund raisers and as warm coverlets for soldiers and anyone to whom the Red Cross gave comfort in 1917 and 1918

resht Inlaid appliqué named after the Iranian city of Resht

retting The process of producing fibre from plant material, usually flax

reverse appliqué Cutwork appliqué; the top fabric is cut through and sewn down to reveal the fabrics layered underneath

Sampler quilt Different block designs set together to create a quilt; frequently employed as a method of learning how to do patchwork

sashiko Japanese form of quilting with white thread on a dark blue ground

satin A fabric with a rich lustre

Seminole Patchwork method, developed by the Seminole of Florida, in which strips of fabric are joined, then cut into segments and rejoined to form patterns

shisha or *abla* Small pieces of mirror glass used on textiles throughout India, Pakistan and parts of Afghanistan

shyrdak Counterchange felt used in the inlay appliqué technique

Signature quilt Quilts dating from the mid-19th century that bear a large number of signatures

Somerset patchwork Folded mitred patchwork recorded in Britain in the 1970s

strippy quilt Made of alternating coloured strips of fabric, running lengthwise, generally quilted with patterns that follow the strips

substantive dyes A dye that does not require the use of a mordant to make it permanent

Suffolk Puffs A fragile, three-dimensional patchwork made by gathering up circles of fabric and sewing them to each other; also known as Yo-Yos

szur The large felt or skin coat worn in rural Hungary

tapa Barkcloth

template Shape cut out of paper, card or plastic to mark out a pattern

Thrift quilt Patchwork quilt made from recycled clothing and furnishings

tivaivai Specific to eastern Polynesia, there are three different quilt forms which all share floral themes that are representational or naturalistic

toran Traditional doorway hanging, India

trade cloth New and second-hand cloth sent from Britain to the colonies in the 19th century

trapunto Stuffed and padded quilting; also known as bas-relief

Tumbling Blocks A box or cube pattern often found in English patchwork, worked with equilateral triangles

Turkey Red The most brilliant of all scarlet red dyes and the most stable

Utility quilt A simply made quilt for everyday use

velvet A cut warp-pile fabric, in which the cut ends form the surface of the fabric

wadding Filling, stuffing or batting: the middle layer of a quilt

waggas Australian indigenous quilts, made from food sacks, cut down clothing or woollen samples

warp The lengthways threads in a woven fabric

weft The widthways threads in a woven fabric

Wholecloth quilt Quilt whose top is made up of lengths of the same fabric, seamed together, usually plain in colour

Yo-Yos *see* Suffolk Puffs

yurt *see* ger

AUSTRALIA
Adelaide
National Textile Museum of Australia
Urrbrae House
Fullarton Road
Urrbrae, Adelaide, South Australia 5064
T (08) 8303 6728

Canberra
National Gallery of Australia
Parkes Place
Parkes, Canberra 2601
T (61) 2 6240 6502
http://www.nga.gov.au/

Victoria
Queenscliffe Historical Museum Inc.
49 Hesse Street
Queenscliffe, Victoria 3225
T (03) 5258 2511

BANGLADESH
Dhaka
Bangladesh National Museum
Shahbag, Dhaka 1000
T 80 2 8619396 9
http://www.bangladeshmuseum.org/

BRITISH ISLES
Bath
The American Museum in Britain
Claverton Manor
Bath BA2 7BD
T 01225 460503
http://www.americanmuseum.org/

Beamish
Beamish, The North of England Open Air Museum
Beamish
County Durham DH9 0RG
T 0191 370 4000
http://www.beamish.org.uk/

Cardiff
St Fagans National History Museum
Cardiff CF5 6XB
T (029) 2057 3500
http://www.museumwales.ac.uk/en/stfagans/

Holywood
Ulster Folk and Transport Museum
153 Bangor Road
Cultra, Holywood, Co. Down
Northern Ireland BT18 0EU
T 028 9042 8428
http://www.uftm.org.uk/

Kendal
Levens Hall
Kendal, Cumbria LA8 0PD
T 015395 60321
http://www.levenshall.co.uk/

London
The British Museum
Great Russell Street
London WC1B 3DG
T 020 7323 8299
http://www.thebritishmuseum.ac.uk/

The Victoria and Albert Museum
Cromwell Road
London SW7 2RL
T 020 7942 2000
http://www.vam.ac.uk/

Manchester
The Whitworth Art Gallery
The University of Manchester
Oxford Road
Manchester M15 6ER
T 0161 275 7450
http://www.whitworth.man.ac.uk/

York
York Castle Museum
Eye of York, York YO1 9RY
T 01904 687687
http://www.yorkcastlemuseum.org.uk/

CANADA
Montreal
McCord Museum of Canadian History
690 Sherbrooke Street West
Montreal, Quebec H3A 1E9
T (514) 398 7100
http://www.musee-mccord.qc.ca/en/

Toronto
Textile Museum of Canada
55 Centre Avenue
Toronto, Ontario M5G 2H5
T (416) 599 5321
http://www.textilemuseum.ca/

CHINA
Beijing
Museum of the Cultural Palace of Minorities
49 Fu Xing Men Nei Road
Xi Cheng District, Beijing 100031
T 86 (0)10 6601 6806
http://www.chinamuseums.com/cultural_palace.htm

DENMARK
Copenhagen
The National Museum (The Prince's Palace)
Ny Vestergade 10
Copenhagen
T (45) 33 13 44 11
http://www.natmus.dk/

FRANCE
Lyon
Musée des Tissus et des Arts Décoratifs
30–34 rue de Charité
69002 Lyon
T 04 78 38 42 00
http://www.musee-des-tissus.com/

Mulhouse
Musée de l'Impression sur Etoffes
14 rue Jean-Jacques Henner
68072 Mulhouse
T (0)3 89 46 83 00
www.musee-impression.com/

GERMANY
Krefeld
German Textile Museum (Deutsches Textilmuseum)
Andreasmarkt 8
47809 Krefeld
T 02151 94694 50
http://www.krefeld.de/

INDIA
Ahmedabad
Calico Museum of Textiles
Sarabhai House
Shahi Baug, 380004 Ahmedabad
Gujarat
http://www.thebharat.com/tourism/museum/
amhadabad.html

Shreyas Folk Museum
Ahmedabad
Gujarat

JAPAN
Osaka
Museum of Dyeing (Kanebo Sen'i Museum)
1–5–102 Tomobuchi-cho
Miyakojima-Ku
Osaka
T 06 6923 4625

THE NETHERLANDS
Arnhem
Open Air Museum (Nederlands Openluchtmuseum)
Schelmseweg 89
6816 SJ Arnhem
T 026 3576111
http://www.openluchtmuseum.nl/

NEW ZEALAND
Wellington
Museum of New Zealand (Te Papa Tongarewa)
Cable Street
Wellington
T 04 381 7000
http://www.tepapa.govt.nz/Tepapa/

NORWAY
Oslo
Museum of Cultural History (Kulturhistorisk Museum)
University of Oslo
Frederiks Gate 2
0164 Oslo
T 22859912
http://www.khm.uio.no/

SWEDEN
Gothenburg
Göteborgs Stadsmuseum
Norra Hamngaten 12
41114 Gothenburg
T 031 61 27 70
http://www.stadsmuseum.goteborg.se/

Stockholm
Museum of Ethnography (Etnografiska Museet)
Djurgardsbrunnsvägen 34
10252 Stockholm
T 08 519 550 00
http://www.etnografiska.se/

UNITED STATES OF AMERICA
Boston
Museum of Fine Arts
Avenue of the Arts
465 Huntingdon Avenue
Boston, MA 02115
T 617 267 9300
http://www.mfa.org/

Cleveland
The Cleveland Museum of Fine Art
University Circle
11150 East Boulevard
Cleveland, OH 44106–1797
T 216 421 7350
http://www.clevelandart.org/

Lancaster
Lancaster Quilt and Textile Museum
37 Market Street
Lancaster, PA 17603
T 717 299 6440
http://www.quiltandtextilemuseum.com/

Lowell
New England Quilt Museum
18 Shattuck Street
Lowell, MA 01852
T 978 452 4207
http://www.nequiltmuseum.org/

New York
American Folk Art Museum
45 West 53rd Street
New York, NY 10019
T 212 265 1040
http://www.folkartmuseum.org/

Cooper-Hewitt National Design Museum
Museum Mile
2 East 91st Street
New York, NY 10128
T 212 849 8400
http://ndm.si.edu/

The Metropolitan Museum of Art
1000 Fifth Avenue at 82nd Street
New York, NY 10028–0198
T 212 535 7710
http://www.metmuseum.org/

Paducah
Museum of the American Quilter's Society
215 Jefferson Street
Paducah, KY 42001
T 270 442 8856
http://www.quiltmuseum.org/

San Jose
San Jose Museum of Quilts and Textiles
520 South First Street
San Jose, CA 95113
T 408 971 0323
http://www.sjquiltmuseum.org/

Santa Fe
Museum of International Folk Art
Museum Hill
706 Camino Lejo
Santa Fe, NM 87505
T 505 476 1200
http://www.moifa.org/

Washington
Textile Museum
2320 S Street, N.W.
Washington, DC 20008–4088
T 202 667 0441
http://www.textilemuseum.org/

BIBLIOGRAPHY

GENERAL

Askari, N., and R. Crill, *Colours of the Indus: Costumes and Textiles of Pakistan*, London, 1997

Clarke, M. C., *Collectible Quilts*, Philadelphia, 1994

Colby, A., *Quilting*, London and New York, 1987

Crill, R., *Indian Embroidery*, London, 1999

Cross, M. Bywater, *Quilts and Women of the Mormon Migrations: Treasures of Transition*, Nashville, Tennessee, 1996

Fitzrandolph, M., *Traditional Quilting: Its Story and Its Practice*, London, 1954

Gillow, J., and B. Sentence, *World Textiles: A Visual Guide to Traditional Techniques*, London and New York, 1999; reprinted 2005

Gostelow, M., *Embroidery: Traditional Designs, Techniques and Patterns from all over the World*, London, 1978, and New York, 1983

Hake, E., *English Quilting, Old and New*, London, 1937; reprinted 1988

Ickis, M., *The Standard Book of Quilt Making and Collecting*, New York, 1949

Paine, S., *Embroidered Textiles: Traditional Patterns from Five Continents with a Worldwide Guide to Identification*, London and New York, 1990

Parker, M. S., *The Folkwear Book of Ethnic Clothing: Easy Ways to Sew and Embellish Fabulous Garments from Around the World*, New York, 2002

Rae, J., *The Quilts of the British Isles*, London, 1987

Rae, J., and D. Travis, *Making Connections: Around the World with Log Cabin*, Chartham, 2004

Rae, J., et al., *Quilt Treasures of Great Britain: The Heritage Search of the Quilters' Guild*, Nashville, Tennessee, 1995

Wilson, N., *Heart of West Africa: Textiles and Global Issues: a Practical and Educational Art and Citizenship Resource*, Derby, 2001

MATERIALS

Argent, J., *Imaginative Leatherwork*, Newton Abbot and South Brunswick, New Jersey, 1975

Attwater, W. A., *Leathercraft*, London, 1961

Collier, A. M., *A Handbook of Textiles*, Oxford and New York, 1974 and 1980

Gaddis, W. (ed.), *A Pile Fabric Primer: Corduroy, Velveteen, Velvet*, New York, 1970

Hall, A. J., *A Student's Textbook of Textile Science*, London, 1963

Hargrave, H., *From Fiber to Fabric*, Lafayette, California, 1997

Mankin, I., and G. Moore, *Natural Fabrics: Simple and Stylish Soft Furnishings*, London, 1997

Mercer, J., *The Spinner's Workshop*, Dorchester, 1978

Miller, E., *Textiles: Properties and Behaviour*, London, 1968

Peachey, S., *Textiles and Materials of the Common Man and Woman, 1580–1660*, Stuart Press, 2001

Robinson, S., *A History of Dyed Textiles: Dyes, Fibres, Painted Bark, Batik, Starch-resist, Discharge, Tie-dye, Further Sources for Research*, London, 1969

Robinson, S., *A History of Printed Textiles: Block, Roller, Screen, Design Dyes, Fibres, Discharge, Resist, Further Sources for Research*, London, 1969

Rothstein, N., *Silk Designs of the Eighteenth Century in the Collection of the Victoria and Albert Museum, London*, London and Boston, 1990

Wells, K., *Fabric Dyeing & Printing*, London and Loveland, Colorado, 1997

USES

Broadbent, M., *Animal Regalia*, Surrey, 1985

Clarke, D., *The Art of African Textiles*, San Diego, California, 1997, and Hoo, 2002

Garrett, V. M., *Traditional Chinese Clothing in Hong Kong and South China, 1840–1980*, Oxford, New York and Hong Kong, 1987

Gillow, J., *African Textiles*, London and San Francisco, 2003

Gillow, J., and N. Barnard, *Traditional Indian Textiles*, London and New York, 1991

Harvey, J., *Traditional Textiles of Central Asia*, London and New York, 1996

Historic Hungarian Costume from Budapest, exh. cat., The Whitworth Art Gallery, Manchester, 1979

Kennett, F., *World Dress*, London, 1994

Kwasnik, E. I. (ed.), *Bulgaria: Tradition and Beauty*, Liverpool, 1989

Lewis, P. W., and E., *Peoples of the Golden Triangle: Six Tribes in Thailand*, London and New York, 1984 and 1998

O'Keeffe, L., *Shoes: A Celebration of Pumps, Sandals, Slippers and More*, New York, 1996

Sheppard, J., *Through the Needle's Eye*, York, 2005

Spring, C., and J. Hudson, *North African Textiles*, London and Washington, D.C., 1995

Taylor, C. F., *Native American Arts and Crafts*, London, 1995

Warner, P., *Embroidery: A History*, London, 1991

Zaman, N., *The Art of Kantha Embroidery*, Dacca, Bangladesh, 1981

Zaman, N., *The Art of Kantha*, Dhaka, 1994

CONSTRUCTION

Bawden, J., *The Art and Craft of Appliqué*, London and New York, 1991

Bishop, R., and E. Safanda, *Amish Quilts*, London, 1976

Chainey, B., *The Essential Quilter: Tradition, Techniques, Design, Patterns and Projects*, Newton Abbot, 1993

Clabburn, P., *Patchwork*, Aylesbury, 1983

Colby, A., *Patchwork*, London, 1976

Corrigan, G., *Miao Textiles from China*, London and Seattle, 2001

Dong-Hwa, H., *Traditional Korean Wrapping Cloths*, Seoul, 1990

Edwards, L., *Through the Window and Beyond: New Designs for Cathedral Window*, Bothell, Washington, 1995

Fox, S., *Wrapped in Glory: Figurative Quilts and Bedcovers, 1700–1900*, London and Los Angeles, 1990

Herald, J., *Exploring Contemporary Quiltmaking*, London, 1993

Hulbert, A., *The Complete Crazy Patchwork: from Victorian Beginnings to Contemporary Design*, London, 2002

Jones, M. E., *A History of Western Embroidery*, London and New York, 1969

Kergreis, S., *French Trapunto*, Kenthurst, Victoria, 1997

Leon, E., *Who'd a Thought It: Improvisation in African-American Quiltmaking*, exh. cat., San Francisco, 1987

Mathews, K., *Molas!: Patterns, Techniques, Projects for Colourful Appliqué*, Asheville, North Carolina, 1998

Muntus, R., *Sashiko: A Japanese Sewing Technique*, Rosemary & Thyme, 1988

Notes on Applied Work and Patchwork, London, 1949

Parker, Mary S., *Sashiko: Easy and Elegant Designs for Decorative Machine Embroidery*, Tunbridge Wells, 2002

Patera, C., *Mola Techniques for Today's Quilters*, Paducah, Kentucky, 1995

Peacey, M., *Mola: Appliqué with a Difference*, Cape Town, 1989

Poggioli, V., *Patterns from Paradise: The Art of Tahitian Quilting*, Pittstown, New Jersey, 1988

Puls, H., *Textiles of the Kuna Indians of Panama*, Princes Risborough, 1988

Rush, B., with L. Wittman, *Complete Book of Seminole Patchwork*, New York, 1993

Wright, M. K., *Folded Star: Mitred Patchwork*, New York, 1986

ARTICLES

Belle Armoire Magazine, Summer 2002 and Winter 2002

Embroidery Magazine, Winter 1965, Summer 1986 (J. Doel), Spring 1993, September 2003 (J. Hemmings) and March–April 2005 (M. Sleigh)

Fibrearts Magazine, March–April 2004 (W. Doe) and September–October 2004 (S. Patterson)

Piecework Magazine, November–December 1993 (T. Faubion), September–October 1994 and May–June 1995 (D. Downs and B. Rush)

Quilt Studies: The Journal of the British Quilt Study Group, Issue 1, 1999

The Quilter Magazine, Summer 1996 (C. Spring), Summer 1997 (L. Dalby), Winter 2001 (M. MacDowell), Autumn 2002 (S. Hallam), Winter 2002 (P. Collingwood and A. Gero) and Winter 2005 (J. Leeb-du Toit)

Selvedge, Issue 05, April–May 2005

Threads Magazine, October–November 1988 (E. Leon)

The World of Embroidery Magazine, November 1998 (K. Smith-Dinn), September 1999 (J. Hughes) and July 2000 (A. Ridge)

INDEX

Photographic credits

a above; *b* below; *c* centre; *d* detail; *i* inset; *l* left; *r* right; *t* top [All studio photography by Tessa Bunney unless otherwise stated]

Afghan Aid 11*br*, 58*b*, 99*tl*, 122*bl*; The American Museum in Britain 119; Meg Andrews (photos David Giles) 15*cr*, 16*bl*, 24*l*, 28*al*, 28*bl*, 28*br*, 30*t*, 30*i*, 44*ar*, 46*bl*, 51*ar*, 90 all, 91 all, 95*c*, 99*cr*, 134*br*, 137*br*, 145*br*; Sue Aspinall 10*tl*, 34*bc*, 40*br*, 43*i*, 74*l* (photo Tessa Bunney), 132*tl*, 149*bl*; Caroline Bevan 36*bl*, 37*cr*, 37*bc*, 89*tr*; Gene Bowen 125*cl*, 138*tl*, 171*tl*, 171*i*; The British Museum 121*br*; Tessa Bunney 79*tl*, 106, 123*tr*, 134*tl*, 177*tl*; Mary Cooper 7*r*, 100, 101, 114, 115, 123*bl*; Caroline Crabtree 13*tr*, 15*bc*, 17*br*, 23, 34*r*, 35*tl*, 35*tc*, 35*br*, 39*bl*, 48, 62, 64*r*, 67, 69*br*, 75*bc*, 80, 81, 93, 96*b*, 123*br*, 132*tr*, 146, 147, 149*tc*, 149*tr*, 150*tl*, 151*tl*, 157*tr*, 158*b*, 161*bl*, 162*b*, 162*i*, 182*tr*; Jean Douglas 15*tr*, 34*l*, 83*bl*, 83*r*; Esther Fitzgerald 107*br*, 113*bl*, 113*br*, 155*bl*, 178; Jim and Diane Gaffney 2, 13*bl*, 22*tl*, 50*tr*, 68*tl*, 84*br*, 85*tl*, 94*t*, 94*b*, 94*i*, 95*bl*, 95*br*, 159*t*, 159*c*, 159*i*, 160*r*; John Gillow 1, 7*bl*, 14, 15*br*, 16*c*, 16*br*, 18*cr*, 19*t*, 21*b*, 22*tr*, 27*t*, 37*tl*, 38*bl*, 49*br*, 59*r*, 60*tl*, 65*tr*, 66*tr*, 66*b*, 69*tl*, 70*tl*, 70*tr*, 83*tr*, 84*t*, 87*t*, 88*tl*, 89*tl*, 92*b*, 95*t*, 96*t*, 97*bl*, 102*l*, 103, 105*tl*, 105*br*, 112*l*, 120, 122*t*, 122*br*, 123*tl*, 124, 130, 131, 132*bl*, 132*br*, 133, 139*tl*, 139*bl*, 140*r*, 141, 149*br*, 154, 156*b*, 160*l*, 160*i*, 161*br*, 169*t*, 183*l*; Joss Graham Gallery 6*br*, 8*tl*, 25*tl*, 27*br*, 29 both, 31*br*, 33*bl*, 35*tr*, 36*bl*, 40*bl*, 59*l*, 60*r*, 61*t*, 63*b*, 65*l*, 66*tl*, 78*b*, 79*b*, 86*l*, 87*b*, 97*tl*, 104, 105*b*, 107*l*, 109*tl*, 109*tr*, 110, 117, 121*t*, 152*r*, 155*tl*, 155*tr*, 163*b*, 166*tr*, 168*tc*, 168*d*; Denise Holtby 11*bl*; Jennifer Hughes 6*tr*, 9*l*, 10*bl*, 10*r*, 12*bl*, 13*cr*, 20*tl*, 20*tr*, 20*br*, 21*t*, 41*br*, 45*tl*, 49*tr*, 68*br*, 71*tl*, 72*r*, 74*r*, 79*tr*, 79*i*, 84*bl*, 85*tc*, 85*tr*, 85*bl*, 85*r*, 88*br*, 89*bl*, 89*br*, 94*cl*, 98*br*, 125*tl*, 125*tr*, 125*cr*, 126*br*, 127*bl*, 134*tl*, 140*t*, 140*bl*, 161*tl*, 161*tc*, 161*tr*, 170*tr*, 174*br*, 175*tl*, 182*bc*, 182*br*, 183*tr*; Hull University, Centre for South-East Asian Studies 13*tl*; Jan Jefferson 138*tr*, 138*bl*, 138*br*; Glenn Jowitt 148, 149*tl*, 169*b*; Leeds City Museum 9*tr*, 12*tl*, 50*bl*, 51*bl*, 97*tr*, 113*tl*, 113*d*, 113*tr*, 145*cr*, 163*tl*, 167*tl*, 167*bl*; Polly Medley 8*bl*, 17*bl*, 46*tr*, 76*br*, 167*r*, 167*d*; Anna Miskin 11*t*, 73*tl*, 150*tr*, 150*br*; Brigid Ockleton 3*c*, 5, 6*l*, 7*tl*, 9*br*, 18*l*, 18*tr*, 18*br*, 26, 30*b*, 32*l*, 38*tr*, 39*l*, 42*tl*, 42*bl*, 43*tl*, 43*tr*, 46*tl*, 47*t*, 49*tc*, 54, 55*t*, 55*l*, 55*b*, 56*tl*, 57, 58*tl*, 76*l*, 77*t*, 82*tl*, 82*r*, 108*b*, 116, 127*tr*, 128, 129, 135*b*, 136 all insets, 137*t*, 145*bl*, 153*t*, 164, 165, 166*b*, 166*d*, 168*l*, 170*bl*, 170*bc*, 171, 172*b*, 173*bl*, 176*r*, 176*d*, 177*b*, 179, 180, 184; Margaret Pettit 56*bl*, 170*bl*; Gordon Reece 157*bl*; Bryan Sentance 118*bl*; Christine Shaw 9*br*, 42*tr*, 44*br*, 69*tr*, 72*l*, 73*br*, 76*r*, 78*tc*, 78*tr*, 92*tr*, 99*bl*, 125*br*, 126*bl*, 135*t*, 143, 145*tr*, 151*bl*, 152*tl*, 156*t*, 157*br*, 158*t*, 168*b*, 174*tr*, 174*cl*, 176*tl*, 177*tr*, 182*tl*, 182*c*, 183*br*; Ron Simpson 31*tr*, 33*cl*, 33*tr*, 49*bc*, 56*tr*, 107*tl*, 107*i*, 109*b*; Kate Smith 43*b*, 52, 53, 58*i*, 136*c*, 137*bl*, 173*r*; Sheila Smith 16*tr*, 24*tr*, 24*br*, 25*br*, 27*c*, 27*br*, 44*cl*, 45*t*, 45*cr*, 63*t*, 70*bl*, 70*br*, 71*bl*, 75*bl*, 86*r*, 139*tr*, 139*br*, 162*tr*; Sally Stone 77*b*, 157*tl*; Victoria and Albert Museum, London 8*tr*, 11*tl*, 12*cl*, 37*br*, 102*l*, 142; Whitby Museum 61*b*; York Castle Museum 24*cr*, 33*tl*, 41*tl*, 47*b*, 50*tl*, 75*t*, 118*tr*, 144, 153*b*, 153*i*